Sue

Amanda

November
2005.

80 Days At Sea
The True Story of a World Cruise

Amanda Wilkins

authorHOUSE™

1663 LIBERTY DRIVE, SUITE 200
BLOOMINGTON, INDIANA 47403
(800) 839-8640
WWW.AUTHORHOUSE.COM

© 2005 Amanda Wilkins. All Rights Reserved.

No part of this book may be reproduced, stored in a retrieval system, or transmitted by any means without the written permission of the author.

First published by AuthorHouse 10/05/05

ISBN: 1-4208-8260-0 (sc)

Printed in the United States of America
Bloomington, Indiana

This book is printed on acid-free paper.

By the same author:

WRITING FROM EXPERIENCE

ROLLER SKATES AND RACKETS

PEVENSEY & WALLSEND

FOR JANET
Who put up with me for three months,
shared my laughter and my tears
and has remained my friend on my return.

and

FOR CHRIS
Who puts up with me at home and
held the fort so well whilst I was away.

My thanks goes to both of them.
Without their support and
encouragement there would
not have been a book.

ACKNOWLEDGEMENTS
This book would not have been
possible without the help I received from
Personal Service Travel, Hailsham,
Haven Life Magazine, The Harbourside,
Newhaven, Zeta Colour, Seaford and
Mr and Mrs Alan Edgar.

PROLOGUE

This is the story of a dream.

A dream that was conceived when I was seventeen years old and came to fruition forty years later. It was a dream that did not turn out quite as expected but I have no regrets at following it.

I have always loved the sea and when my parents first took me cruising on the P & O liner Oronsay in my late teens I knew one day I had to sail round the world.

In 2005 I achieved that dream on the new Oriana..A World Cruise is everybody's fantasy if they like the sea. Months of luxury, glamour and excitement – or so I thought when I boarded the huge white liner in Southampton on a cold, wet January afternoon.

Little did I know that day that it would not all be "a bowl of cherries."

There were good days, more good than bad. But there were also days. – and nights – when I suffered bouts of acute loneliness in a world inhabited by couples.

A hint of romance brought on by the heady atmosphere of sunsets and turquoise seas turned out to be one-sided and left me feeling frustrated and the sheer boredom of the repetitive routine on board, especially during the long spells at sea, severely raised the stress levels.

On the bad days the luxury liner didn't seem quite so luxurious when it had been your home for nearly three months, the claustrophobic atmosphere became more like a prison and made you wish you could meet your friends back home in the local pub.

But I have no regrets about going as my memories will remain with me forever. The moment we sailed into Sydney and I saw the opera house and the harbour bridge for the first time and the wonderful performance of Carmen I saw in the evening.

The friendliness of the people of Tonga and the beautiful beach at Pago Pago, the real home of Somerset Maugham's heroine Sadie Thompson. Walking round a corner in Hong Kong and seeing the famous dragon dance and the hollow feeling in my stomach when I saw the utter devastation caused by the tsunami in Phuket.

It was a trip that changed my life forever. This is my story of Eighty Days at sea.

DAYS ONE and TWO
Shake, Rattle and Roll.

Travel is like sex.

Embarking on any new relationship or journey is a gamble and the first few days might not live up to expectations. But if you care enough you persist and disappointment fades into oblivion.

That was how I felt when I set out from Southampton on January 7th 2005 to follow in the footsteps of Phineas Fogg.

When I planned my round the world trip in July 2004 I had not realized it would take 80 days. It only dawned on me two months after I had booked the trip – and that added to the excitement engendered throughout the planning stage.

I was brought up on the Jules Verne classic and I had been glued to my television screen watching Michael Palin travelling round the world in 80 days by train – now I was going to do it by ship, so why not write about my adventures. No woman had done it before.

Travelling alone I decided to do it in diary form – Bridget Jones meets Jules Verne.

When I sold my flat in Eastbourne to move along the coast to Newhaven I decided not to buy – I wanted to travel, see the world before I was too old and infirm to enjoy it.

I took a tiny bed-sitting room with no hot water and a damp shower room for a minimal rent and counted the days to departure.

Just like Jules Verne's intrepid hero nearly lost his bet because they forgot the time change I nearly lost the opportunity to follow in his footsteps.

Giving up my flat at the end of December to avoid another month's rent and council tax I was house-sitting for none other than the Mayor of Newhaven. Living in absolute luxury for ten days it was with mixed feelings I left the house when my friends arrived to drive me to Southampton,

Eager to load up the car with my massive amount of luggage I put my handbag in the hall and helped with the cases. The door blew shut behind me with the rest of my luggage, money, passport, travellers cheques and the front door key inside.

My friends and I stared in horror at the locked door. We

walked round the house and tried all the double glazed windows. I tried the next door neighbour – no key.

"The lady across the road has one," she said. "No she doesn't," I replied. "I am due to put it through her letter box when I leave!".

I rang the police – they didn't want to know. Then I remembered a locksmith I knew in the town. My friends drove me there and I threw myself on his mercy. Like a knight in shining armour he arrived on the doorstep within quarter-of-an-hour. Five minutes later he had the door open, charging me £47 for doing so.

On board the massive ship I prepared for the voyage ahead. The band of the Adjutant General's Corps struck up Auld Lang Syne and we were handed a glass of champagne and streamers for our last sight of England for eighty days.

Then we waited, and waited. Fifteen minutes went by and still we didn't move. Captain Mike Carr came on the microphone and said we were heading into a gale in the English Channel but it was nothing to worry about. But still we did not move.

Then eventually the ropes were released and finally, we were underway.

So what was the problem, was there something wrong with

the ship? Not at all. An overenthusiastic lady passenger threw her streamers with great vigour. Unfortunately she had her handbag on the same arm and over it went, right into the water between the quay and the ship.

Crew members tried to retrieve it but were unsuccessful. So the unlucky passenger started off on her trip without her glasses, money and personal possessions.

The Captain was true to his word and we did meet the gale, Force Ten. I sat and watched the massive waves hitting the picture window of my cabin on F deck and regretted I was unable to show off my sporting prowess on the shuffleboard court.

The creaking of the ship made me think back to the days of Admiral Lord Nelson sailing into battle at Trafalgar and I knew I was really at sea..

DAY THREE
For Those in Peril

There is something special about a church service at sea. Held in the Theatre Royal and led by Staff Captain Charlie Carr it was short, to the point and contained all my favourite hymns.

Perhaps the most poignant for the passengers was For Those in Peril on the Sea. Although Oriana had never been in peril we had faced some horrendous weather since we sailed from Southampton.

The wind increased to Gale Force 11 with a very large swell and the passengers were conspicuous by their absence on the decks and in the restaurants.

Only the stalwarts, myself being one of them, remained on their feet and we lurched drunkenly round the ship clutching on to the hand rails and sometimes our fellow passengers. Doors to the outer decks were sealed off by yellow tape and all the swimming pools were closed.

In the last 24 hours we had only sailed a distance of 418

miles and we were hopelessly behind schedule.

Deck sports were abandoned much to the dismay of seasoned cruisers who take their deck quoit competitions very seriously.

Passengers had to make do with inside entertainment ,line dancing, quizzes, an art auction and the shops where we all spent too much money for lack of alternative things to do.

The Captain announced his Welcome Aboard cocktail parties would be put off until we had reached better weather then suddenly things began to change.

The swell got smaller and the wind dropped to Gale Force Seven. Following the daily noon announcement Mike Carr said invitations were being circulated to the cabins to tell passengers his parties would take place after all.

Although this announcement promised better things ahead it caused consternation amongst the ladies'

There was a mad stampede to the hair and beauty salon with people fighting to get appointments. Queues formed outside every ironing room as they waited to iron their best ball gowns, crumpled from days folded up in the suitcases.

Deck games were on hold as the wind was still very strong and the swimming pools were flooding the shuffleboard and quoits court. Tapes remained on the doors of the side decks but the passengers were allowed out onto the top deck if they were brave enough to do so.

Smiles began to appear on the faces of the passengers as they realized the warm Caribbean weather was just around the corner.

Tales of uncomfortable hours spent lying in darkened cabins were swapped across the lunch table as hungry passengers who had starved themselves since leaving Southampton tucked into food now piled high on their plates.

Everyone tried to outdo their neighbour by saying how much worse their seasickness had been and it became a game everyone wanted to win.

A weak sun appeared in an overcast sky and the grey sea became something to watch instead of something to fear.

Evening came and decks were deserted as the passengers prepared for one of the highlights of the cruise – a chance to shake hands and be photographed with the Captain.

Passengers who decided their best frocks were not up to standard visited the Knightsbridge shop to snap up Frank Usher evening gowns at £500 each.

The English are a strange bunch – we will queue for hours

for anything, and that is never more obvious than on a ship.

Long before the appointed time for dinner, where everyone has an allocated table and there is no need to rush, they form an orderly queue outside the dining room as if they are facing their last meal,

The same thing happened for the Captain's cocktail parties. Divided into two sittings, the same as for dinner, each passenger received an invitation and ample time was left for everyone to be admitted..

But sure enough, half an hour before, queues formed outside the door. Dripping with jewels and newly coiffured hairdos, the ladies looked around anxiously to make sure no-one was wearing the same dress.

A ripple of excitement ran through the crowd as the doors opened and they were off, only to be followed by disappointment when they discovered they had gone in the wrong door of the Crows Nest. Expecting to be greeted by Captain Mike Carr they found they were welcomed by Executive Purser Zak Coombs, Captain Carr was the other side!

One seasoned traveller was broken hearted. "This is the first World Cruise I have done where I won't have a photograph of me being welcomed by the Captain," she said, looking even more crestfallen when she was handed over to the Third

Engineer who was to be her host.

With seventy-seven more days to go the atmosphere began to change. Dancing the night away at the Welcome Aboard Ball, people were prepared to get into a holiday mood. The worst of the weather hopefully behind us we were all looking forward to the sunshine ahead.

DAY FOUR
Swing High, Swing Low.

This was the day the passengers had waited for. After many hours spent lying prone on their bunks suffering from seasickness they were due to set foot on terra firma for the first time since leaving England.

At 1pm we were scheduled to arrive in Ponta Delgada in The Azores. One of the most remote and far-flung outposts of Portugal many people were eager to see the highlight of the visit, the two lakes of Seta Citades, a natural wonder in the central mountains.

But no-one can predict the weather and at 12 noon on day four we were still 120 miles away from The Azores, having covered a distance of only 490 miles in 24 hours.

The Captain decided if we were to get to Barbados on time he would have to miss out the port and head straight for the Caribbean island.

Passengers were now faced with seven days at sea without seeing land. But every cloud has a silver lining.

By lunchtime on day four the temperature had risen to 61 degrees and the wind had dropped to gale force four.

The entertainment officers vainly tried to hold the deck competitions, quoits and shuffleboard, but it was very much a question of one step forward and two back. Attempting to play shuffleboard against the wind was nearly impossible and many people decided to leave it for another day.

The sight of the officers donning their "whites" in the afternoon was a sheer sign of warmer weather and a few brave people ventured into the newly-opened Jacuzzis on the open deck.

But despite the promise of better conditions I started to worry. My clothes were beginning to get tighter after three days of cooked breakfasts, lunch and five course dinners and I could see myself being six stone heavier at the end of the trip.

I do not travel in lifts. I suffer from claustrophobia dating back to the time I was shut in a cupboard at kindergarten by a small boy. I was four-and-a-half at the time and don't remember the incident, but my mother said I was trapped for two hours before somebody found me. So from day one I had religiously toiled up and down the stairs from deck five to deck thirteen.

I knew I was getting fitter when I could reach deck thirteen without being breathless and with no aches and pains in my legs, but I also knew it was time to visit the well-equipped gymnasium before the ship sank under my weight.

The sea was still grey, the sky overcast but a circular from the tours office lifted our spirits. It informed us there was till availability on a tour in Barbados to go and swim with the giant turtles and I went to find out more.

"You go by catamaran for an unforgettable adventure," said the young girl on the desk. "You will sail along the island's west coast to a sheltered bay where you can snorkel with a group of wild Sea Turtles."

"There is just one problem," I said. "I can't snorkel." I decided it was not a good time to tell her that I had also booked to sail on an America's Cup yacht in Auckland harbour and I didn't know how to sail either..

But I am game for anything and a quick learner and I had decided I would never again have the opportunity to sail on NZL 40 or NZL 41, whichever one I was allocated to crew for the morning.

It is amazing how quickly you adapt to shipboard life and learn to find your way around. When I boarded the 69,000 ton liner in Southampton I thought I would get hopelessly lost.

Three days out I could find my way from one end of the

ship to the other with no problem at all and I had not been forced to sleep in one of the lounges because I had failed to locate my cabin.

Oriana was the first ever superliner designed for the British passenger and she is elegant and stylish. The seventy-foot waterfall in the atrium looks better as you climb higher and can appreciate its full beauty.

This trip may not have had the excitement of the balloon flight in Jules Verne's novel or the ever-changing scenery experienced by Michael Palin's train journey but one thing it did have was its highs and lows.

In the early hours of the morning of day four I lay on my bed and watched the swelling sea through the window of my cabin. I found myself slipping back into Phineas Fogg's shoes and I wondered if I too was going to have problems achieving my aim.

But with the long-awaited appearance of the sun I began to experience the same excitement felt by Fogg when he set off from London to win his bet and the same excitement Michael Palin must have felt when he started his journey that kept us glued to our television screens for weeks on end.

DAY FIVE
Sunshine and smiles

I was woken on the fifth day

of my round-the-world trip

by a strange light.

A gap in the curtain at the head of my bed prompted me to dress as quickly as I could and go to the open deck. Climbing the stairs to deck 13 I found I was not the only passenger eager to get out in the fresh air to welcome the new day.

The sea was still an ugly shade of grey and I could see a glimmer of a rainbow in the distance over the stern, but ahead the sky looked bluer and brighter as if we were approaching the gates of Heaven.

There was an air of optimism that at last this was the start of our big adventure. A lone jogger dodged in and out of the walkers as we were all eager to take our morning constitutional.

Friendly banter went on among the walkers as to how many

turns round the deck it would take to complete one mile. I did three-and-a-half, satisfied that I had indeed achieved the distance.

For the first time since we left Southampton we could breakfast on deck. I took up the Titanic pose in the stern and like Kate Winslet I did feel I was flying. But sadly there was no Leonardo de Caprio standing behind me to support my waist and lift me on the bars.

I decided day five was the day I would make my cruise debut on the shuffleboard court and I drew Fred J as my partner.

A charming gentleman, he told me when we drew to play against his wife he would have to lose in the first round! But he decided to throw chivalry to the wind and played like a demon taking us right through to the final.

This became a needle match with only one point in it as we prepared to push the wooden chuck down the court for the last time.

It was more by luck than judgement that any of us had got to the final as the wind was still very strong. If you pushed too hard with the paddle the chuck ended up in the minus ten box and if you were too weak it never made the court at all.

But it was all good fun and it was a way of meeting your

fellow passengers. Being soundly beaten on the last round we congratulated our worthy opponents as they received their P & O washbags.

On a cruise there is always a mixed selection of people and I felt sorry for an embarrassed lady I met in the steam room at the health club.

Before she faded out of sight in the gathering steam I saw she was wrapped in a towel that was getting damper by the minute.

"I didn't bring my swimming costume so I have had to borrow my husband's Y-fronts," she said.

She told me she had been to the shop but all they had left was a selection of costumes three sizes too big so until the ship reached Barbados she had to make do with her husband's pants.

Once word gets out you are writing a book everyone wants to be in it. A number of passengers approached me to ask if I was "the lady writer". "I hope you are going to put me in your book, I am very photogenic," one man said.

But it also has its advantages. The entertainment staff collected anecdotes that I might find amusing and one tale about an unfortunate passenger did make me laugh.

A gentleman travelling on his own was prone to

sleepwalking but as he had not experienced any previous problems he decided to go on a leg of the World Cruise.

Two nights out of Southampton, despite the movement of the ship, he walked out of his cabin in his pyjamas, strolled around the decks inside the ship and ended up in Tiffany's lounge on D deck, where there are no passenger cabins.

He was talking quite happily to two startled passengers before he woke up and realized what he had done.

Profusely embarrassed, he apologized and told them he would never be able to go on another cruise. But luckily they all saw the funny side and he has probably made some new lifelong friends after his little adventure.

In the first five days the clocks were put back two hours in two stages so it was difficult to remember what time it was in England.

Phone calls to the UK were expensive, nearly £5 a minute, but if people did have to phone home they had to work out not only what time it was but also how long they could afford to talk for.

Oriana's communications are excellent and no-one is cut off from their friends and families, even in bad weather. The ship's cyb@centre has to be seen to be believed and passengers could hire one hour's internet time for £15.

Life at sea was beginning to become a round of deck sports, betting on the ship's daily run, going to quizzes, watching the shows and eating – breakfast, lunch, tea and dinner. Even a midnight buffet if you so desired. The boredom of the repetitive routine had not yet set in because it was still all so new and exciting and I had so many exotic ports of call to look forward to.

On day five Oriana started to pick up speed steaming a distance of 544 miles since noon the previous day. We were well on course for Barbados having made up the time by missing out Ponta Delgada.

Spirits were rising and postcards were being written in anticipation for our arrival at the Caribbean island in four days time.

But I was thinking even further ahead – to my first ever visit to New Zealand and Australia. I was starting to worry about the sun having been told it would be hotter than I ever imagined.

Being born with red hair I have a very fair skin and I knew my English sun tan lotion would not be sufficient. But on a ship there is always someone to help.

One of the entertainment officers dispatched me to the shop

to get a bottle of P20, the silicone-based sunfilter they all use.

The Oriana Theatre Company staged first class musicals throughout the cruise, only marred by the fact they were repeated on every leg.

The first of these was Fosse, a tribute to Broadway producer Bob Fosse which included excerpts from many familiar shows.

The entertainment was all included in the fare and the shows were worthy of any West

End stage.

The company were friendly and were often to be found on deck between rehearsals.

Having worked in theatre, then theatrical journalism most of my life I always gravitate towards actors and singers and soon several members of the company became firm friends.

DAY SIX
Stop the World

No-one can predict what fate has in store for us and that was never more obvious than six days out of Southampton.

We had braved the storms and rough seas and were now being rewarded with warm sunshine and little wind. Captain Carr had done his usual promenade round the decks informing passengers that we were to have two extra hours in Barbados having missed out Ponta Delgada.

I joined other passengers for my first swim in the open air pool and then relaxed in the Jacuzzi in preparation for a special lunch for those travelling round the world.

But just before 11am fate decided to intervene.

There was a loud bang and the ship shuddered before coming to a standstill.. The crew were called to their action stations and a few minutes later the fire party was called.

The Captain announced there had been a "blow-out" and it had affected our propulsion so we had come to a halt in the middle of the Atlantic, miles from anywhere. He assured the passengers there was nothing for them to worry about and said there was no fire and no-one had been hurt.

It is strange what a bit of sunshine can do to lift the spirits. Shipboard life went on as usual with people sunbathing, swimming and playing deck sports.

The restaurants were closed as the power had gone, so had the lights inside the ship, and the emergency lighting dispelled an eerie gloom everywhere, especially on the lower decks.

The Round the World cocktail party and lunch was postponed for two days and passengers were expecting sandwiches and asking where they were.

It was then the purser's department sprung into action. Crew members carried the barbecue and food up five decks from the galley as the lifts were not working. Within fifteen minutes they had set up a sumptuous barbecue by the swimming pool and soon a long queue formed to sample burgers, steaks and a selection of salads.

For four hours the ship remained stationery, swinging round with the tide, but there was no sense of panic. Having been reassured we were in no danger passengers seemed relieved they could sunbathe without interruption from the vibration of the engines.

How different it would have been if it had happened in the bad weather when we were confined inside the ship

Regular announcements were made assuring the passengers they were trying to find the cause of the problem and the Captain promised to let everyone know when we were underway.

Full lighting was restored within an hour and some of the lifts began to work, which was a great relief to the elderly and infirm passengers on board. We remained without water and air conditioning but that was not a problem as long as we could remain on deck.

Just before 3pm, four hours after the incident which took everyone by surprise, including the Captain, they managed to start the engines manually. Setting off on one propeller and at half speed while they affected repairs we were once again en route for Barbados.

In the evening the Captain kept his word and told everyone over the ship's loudspeaker what had happened to Oriana to stop her in her tracks.

They had been installing a second air conditioning unit because of the rising temperatures and as they were doing so there was a blow-out. This resulted in a total power failure throughout the ship and affected the propulsion of the engines.

My cabin was down on F deck and although it had a large picture window it was uncomfortably hot. As I dressed for dinner I resorted to propping the cabin door open with the waste paper basket..To keep the cost down I was sharing with a stranger, but as soon as I met Janet Graham I knew we wouldn't be strangers for long. A bubbly Scottish lady from Glasgow she had a tremendous sense of humour and we got on from day one.

Janet is a widow and was on her first cruise. She had no idea how she would like it but she came on board prepared to enjoy herself. Our cabin was tiny and if she had the wardrobe door open I could not get in as the cabin door nearly knocked her for six – we had many a laugh about that throughout the three months we were to spend together.

It was supposed to be Ladies Night when the formal evening dresses came out for the first time since the Captain's cocktail party. But because the ship was so hot the Executive Purser decided it was wiser to relieve the men of wearing stifling dinner jackets and make it a casual night when people could dress as they liked. The main object was to keep cool. As a result one of the highlights of the cruise fell flat on its face.

Each leg of the World Cruise attracts different entertainers and travelling from Southampton to San Francisco was poet Pam Ayres who this year is celebrating her 30th anniversary as an entertainer.

Her first performance had to be cancelled as she was ill so it had been rescheduled for the sixth night out. As we went into the Theatre Royal we were handed sheets of paper to use as a fan and told it would be very hot in there.

Pam valiantly took to the stage faced with a sea of waving paper. She was very funny but after 30 minutes the heat became too much and I had to leave.

The higher decks were cooler because all the doors were open and fresh air wafted down the corridors. Several people were walking the decks and some had even settled down for the night on the sunbeds.

I went down to my cabin at 11.15pm to see what it was like but I knew I would not be able to sleep. Returning to the deck I stood there until it became too cold to stay

Deciding to brave it in the cabin I found the air conditioning had begun to work and once again was blessed with a blast of cold air.

The first six days had certainly been eventful and we all began to wonder what else was in store for us as we steamed around the world.

DAY SEVEN
A few dollars more

Approaching Barbados it was now time to think of our plans for the Caribbean island. Before I left England I had decided I must visit Columbian Emeralds in Bridgetown – not that I expected to be able to afford any of the precious stones. But I had promised myself one day I would buy myself an emerald ring..

My excursion to snorkel with the Giant Turtles was not scheduled to leave the ship until 1.15pm and as we were due to dock at 8am, I would have time to do my shopping first.

Deciding to approach the bureau before a crowd gathered to change my sterling travellers cheques into dollars, I was delighted to find the exchange rate was so good. I got $1.80 for each pound I exchanged.

There were also the obligatory postcards to write and I felt I ought to send a multiple email back home. I run a magazine with my business partner Chris Morgan and I had left him in charge so the least I could do was send him a message.

I had telephoned him during the bad weather via the ship's satellite system but it had taken three goes to get through. Twice I could hear his voice but he couldn't hear me and when he answered in a very irritated tone at the third attempt he said he could barely hear me. At £4.95 a minute it had been a pointless and expensive exercise.

Every passenger receives a daily paper Oriana Today which becomes your bible. It tells you everything that is happening in the ship and you are constantly checking it to see where you are supposed to be.

We also received an abbreviated Daily Mail produced exclusively for P & O ships. Since we left Southampton it had been full of doom and gloom back home in England. 120 mile per hour storms, floods and murders.

On the seventh day of our trip I read that experts were warning that hundreds of thousands of people would be struck down by a major flu epidemic in the next few weeks.

Cases of flu-like illnesses in the UK had hit their highest level since the season started in October and were expected to peak in the first week of February. I was very glad I was away from it all, basking in the Caribbean sunshine.

For the first time since we sailed Dirk Klopper, the South African senior doctor and his medical team were able to come out on deck together to enjoy a buffet lunch.

I asked him if his busy period was over and he said the next thing he would be treating would be sunburn. He warned me to be very careful, especially in Australia and New Zealand.

My life had become a routine of breakfast on deck with Janet before went our separate ways, entering the shuffleboard competition, the game on which I was completely hooked, going to the individual quiz and betting on the ship's daily run.

I had won none of the above, but I had reached the final of the shuffleboard competition twice so there was hope I might win a selection of P & O wash bags to bring home to Southampton.

Following lunch on deck I would go back to the shuffleboard court before trying my hand at Jackpot bingo. At £5 a day it was becoming an expensive gamble but my heart was set on winning the snowball jackpot in the last game. On day seven it stood at £1,200 which you could win if you got a full house in 50 numbers so it was still worth a try.

Dinner was always in the restaurant and the dress code varied according to the evening's entertainment. There was plenty of variety for everyone ranging from quizzes, films, cabarets and dancing.

There was also the casino. At 50p a bet on the roulette table it was great fun and something I could not afford to do at home. Blackjack and poker were a bit more restrictive if you were doing the full 80 days with the minimum bet being £3.

Sunshine brings out the best in people and the troubles of the past few days were forgotten. A few bad jokes were made about the sound of the engines and how we would be at sea forever.

But in the 18 hours since we started after our breakdown Oriana had managed to steam a distance of 474 miles. This was a remarkable achievement as part of that time was at half speed and a credit to Captain Carr and his team of officers.

DAY EIGHT
Pantomime and Port

It seemed hard to believe that just one week ago we were travelling down to Southampton to board the Oriana. It felt as if we had been on board for weeks

Emails from home informed us that Oriana had made the national press due to her exploits in the Atlantic,. and the Captain announced that he had not been able to make up the time following the breakdown and a heavy swell after we got started again.

We would therefore be alongside at Barbados at 10.30am on January 15 instead of 8am and he expected the ship to be cleared for passengers to go ashore at 11.30am.

A note in my cabin informed me that due to lack of response my excursion to swim with the Giant Turtles had been cancelled but because of our late arrival I was not too disappointed as I wanted to explore Bridgetown. I was just looking forward to stepping ashore after so long at sea.

The 800 passengers travelling around the world had been

invited to a special cocktail party and lunch. Some had been invited the previous day but it was my turn on day eight, rescheduled from the day we broke down.

We were told to go to the Pacific Lounge at 12 noon where we were greeted by the Captain. Admitting I had forgotten my invitation he sent me back down to my cabin to get it otherwise he said I would get no lunch!

Wine flowed freely, white, red and afterwards there was a choice of port or brandy.

The choice of sweets included crepe suzette which was lit for us by the chef and it was a very happy bunch who staggered out of the restaurant just after 2pm.

I discovered it was not a good idea to play shuffleboard when you had been imbibing. Having reached three finals since Southampton, and winning none of them, I crashed miserably out of the competition in the first round following my lunch.

There was no other choice after my dismal failure but to go to the cabin and sleep off the celebrations before getting into formal attire for the evening.

The entertainment programme had been changed considerably since we left Southampton with very little scheduled evening entertainment taking place on the appointed day.

This was due to the inclement weather when it was too dangerous for the dancers to perform, and the breakdown of the air conditioning which meant every public room became uncomfortably hot.

Now with things getting back to normal the evening we had all been looking forward to could at last take place.

On the eighth day out of Southampton the Theatre Company had the opportunity to have as much fun as the audience in the packed Theatre Royal.

On the Christmas and New Year cruises they had performed their potted version of Aladdin.

Now, on day eight of the world cruise, they were performing the show again and none of us were disappointed.

It was a mixture of music, laughter, adventure and audience participation. Backed by the Keith Trewitt Orchestra it was as good as any pantomime you would see on shore.

A very happy group of passengers went to bed with the sound of "Oh no it isn't" ringing in their ears and looking forward to the following day and their first port of call.

DAY NINE
BARBADOS

A ripple of excitement ran round the whole ship when we spotted our first sight of land for nine days.

Barbados was clearly visible in the morning mist and binoculars to the fore people lined the decks three deep watching as we got nearer and nearer.

Watchful eyes tried to see who could be first to spot the pilot boat, looking like a toy against the hull of the huge white liner. It drew alongside and with great skill the Basian pilot was up the ladder and making his way to the bridge.

Barbados is the most easterly island in the West Indies with the powerful Atlantic Ocean on its east coast and the clear, calm waters of the Caribbean Sea on the south and west coasts.

The island measures just 21 square miles and 14 miles at its widest point so a lot of passengers booked the half day tour round the island.

I had visited Barbados twice before and the first time I was taken on a tour by a local resident so I decided, due to our late arrival, I would walk into Bridgetown.

We should have been alongside at 8am, instead we arrived just after 11am and passengers were not allowed ashore until the officials had cleared the ship.

When we docked they were on board the Star Clipper, a magnificent four-masted sailing ship moored just in front of us so we had to wait for clearance.

Even though they work at a slower pace in the Caribbean we were still able to go ashore at 11.30am and I walked to the terminal building where a plethora of enticing shops selling tax free goods waited for us.

Ignoring the usual souvenirs I used to buy as a child I went straight to Columbian Emeralds, famous in the Caribbean for its luscious green stones sold at very reasonable prices.

Before I left England I had made a list of things I wanted to take back and an emerald ring was top of my list. I was served by a young Basian, also called Amanda, who asked what my budget was. She then went to endless trouble to find "something special" and I left the shop clutching my precious emerald and diamond ring, together with a Certificate of Authentication.

Having been with so many people for so long I wanted to be on my own, and Barbados is a place where in the daytime a lone female can feel perfectly safe.

During the twenty minute walk from the Terminal to the town centre I was greeted with smiles and handshakes. When I said I did not want a taxi I was not pestered but told if I changed my mind that was the car I should choose.

Passing a souvenir stall under a large tree I was asked where my husband was. When I said I hadn't got one I was faced with a huge smile and a display of sparkling white teeth. A hand was extended and gripped mine firmly, "Hi, I'm Clarence, he said."There is my car, let me show you my beautiful island."

The Basians must be the most hospitable people in the world. In every shop I went into I was greeted with a warm welcome and no pressure to buy.

I strolled round the local fruit and vegetable market where I never saw a white face and watched the locals doing their weekly shopping.

When you get into the heart of the capital town you realize at once why it is known throughout the Caribbean as "Little England."

The market-town atmosphere, Georgian houses, Parliament Square and neo-Gothic public buildings all contribute to the impression.

Coming from East Sussex I was fascinated to see signposts

to Hastings and Worthing and from the top deck of the ship I could clearly see the cricket ground and score board, famous for so many test matches.

Heroes Square is the civic heart of the town and the focal point is the statue of Admiral Lord Nelson. It was erected in 1813 on the site of "The Green" where hansom cabs once waited for their fares.

Lord Nelson spent some time in Barbados during his command of naval station at English Harbour, Antigua.

Oriana was not due to sail until midnight so I had plenty of time to explore before walking back to the ship, exhausted from the heat of the day, but happy we had visited such a friendly place.

A treat was in store for the passengers in the evening when the Barbados Tourist Band brought their steel drums on board and gave us an hour's superb entertainment by the swimming pool.

Oriana partied into the night as we set sail from Barbados. We were heading for our next port of call Curacao and it was with a heavy heart I watched the lights of Barbados fade into oblivion. I knew one day I had to return.

DAY TEN
Laziness and Lessons

A day at sea sandwiched between two ports heralds the lazy, hazy days of summer. Recovering from the exertions in Barbados and anticipating the exploration of Curacao prompted several prone bodies to relax on sunbeds round the various pools.

Being very much self taught on my digital camera I decided to sign up for an Oriana Cyb@study course in digital photography.

Reasonably priced at £50 for three two hour sessions I was to be taught everything about my camera and how to edit my photographs.

That was the idea. But the electrical breakdown had turned everything upside down on the ship and on the day of my first lesson all the computers were down.

I was told I had to report for a three-hour lesson on day 10 at 10am. This meant I was unable to attend the church service, this week taken by the Captain, and I had to concentrate inside the ship for three hours instead of being out on deck in the sunshine.

The tutor was excellent and I soon learnt how to re-size, recolour and change the whole texture of my photographs. I even learnt to add special affects and clone a sheep's head on to a cow.

That could come in very useful if I wanted to design a special picture of someone I really disliked.

But the change of time in the heat of the day, despite the air conditioning, took its toll and I ended up with a splitting headache and wondering if I would attend the next lesson. We were even given homework, which is not really compatible with a holiday.

The mental exhaustion of going back to school resulted in a relaxing afternoon in and out of the pool and the jacuzzi on deck.

Oriana offers a wide range of dining facilities and the night after Barbados the Conservatory was transformed into an Indian setting for a special buffet dinner.

As two members of our table were leaving the ship at San Francisco we decided to book for the Indian meal and we were not disappointed.

However tired the entertainment staff must be with things to arrange night after night they came up with a perfect plan to end the day, especially for people of my generation.

The great band on the World Cruise, Powerhouse, headed the team to take us back to the Swinging 60s and the sensational 70s.

Despite partying on deck until the early hours after Barbados there were plenty of people reliving their youth and bopping the night away.

DAY ELEVEN
CURACAO

There are some places that hit you with their beauty from the moment you see them and Curacao is one of them.

Described as "A Little Holland in the West Indies" the people are friendly, there is a wonderful climate and the Caribbean Sea surrounding the island is crystal clear. Curacao is a multi-faceted diamond in the crown of the Netherlands Antilles and you can see the Dutch influence as soon as you visit the capital Willemstad where Oriana docked.

It was a short and pleasant walk into the town centre, and many passengers chose to do that rather than go on an organized tour.

The 17th century gabled houses are painted in a wide range of bright pastel shades, greens, pinks, blues and yellows.

When I woke up on the eleventh day at 7am we were already alongside and I rushed up to the open deck to be faced by lush greenery and colourful facades.

The magnificent road bridge dominated the skyline, in contrast to the Queen Emma Bridge (Koningin Emmabrug) that we had to cross to reach the town centre.

This pontoon bridge stretches across St Anna Bay linking the Punda And the Otrabanda (literally the other side) districts of Willemstad.

It is powered by a diesel engine and swings open several times a day but no-one is stranded as there is a free ferry service operating when the bridge is open.

Our walk into town was lined with souvenir stalls with all their traders urging us to buy from them. But they did not push and if you said no they left you alone.

I thought the Basians were friendly but I soon discovered the welcoming hospitality stretches across the Caribbean. Eager residents wanted to know what the ship was like and how much it cost to travel in her.

Curacao is steeped in history and dates back to 1499 when it was discovered by the Spaniard Alonso de Opeda. The first Spanish settlers arrived in 1527 but the Dutch arrived in 1534 and promptly shipped the Spanish off to Venezuala.

It was the Dutch who changed the name of the capital to Willemstad from Santa Anna and Peter Stuyvesant became Governor in 1642.

I was amused to see a mixture of old and new in the town centre, with the ancient Fort Amsterdam vying with the ultra modern department stores and Kentucky Fried Chicken.

The eighteenth century fort used to be a focal point of the

city, being the most important defence structure on the island. But it is now used by Curacao's administrative seat Government House, and several other administrative offices.

I had intended to tour the island but with an early sailing and so much to see in Willemstad I decided to explore the city.

From the fort I went along to the Fort Church (Fort Kerk). Built in 1742 it is the oldest Protestant Church on the island. By the time I had found it the museum attached to it was shut for lunch but returning at 2pm I was able to go in. From the outside it looked fairly small but inside it was an Aladdin's cave filled with christening robes, costumes, antique silver chalices and other religious memorabilia.

On the other side of the Fort was an even more interesting contrast of ancient and modern, the Water Fort.

Dating from 1534 it now houses modern shops and restaurants in the arches. But there is always someone willing to relay its history and I was told it played a key role in the Second World War.

In partnership with the Rif Fort to the west of Otrabanda a steel net was stretched across the harbour to prevent enemy ships from entering.

All too soon I had to head back to Oriana in preparation for our 6pm sailing. I could easily have spent two days or more exploring Curacao.

It must be the most unique place in the world with its colourful houses, intricate architecture, particularly noticeable on the Raadzaal (town hall) and the Satenzaal which houses the parliament of the Netherlands Antilles.

I was sad to think we were leaving the Caribbean, even though I knew we had more exciting things to come, but I did not return to my temporary home empty handed. My bag was weighed down with two bottles of the island's famous liqueur.

We sailed on time heading for the Panama Canal and as usual the entertainment team sprang into action with a choice of the Great British Pub Night or Gary Williams giving us the Legend of Sinatra, a role he had played in London's West End in The Rat Pack.

But I chose to remain on deck until the last lights of the Caribbean faded into oblivion and it was with a heavy heart I said goodbye to Curacao.

DAY TWELVE
Comedy classic

On the twelfth day of my Round the World adventure I woke up knowing I was suffering from over-indulgence.

Too much sun and too much food so I knew I had to spend a day out of the sun. I decided to go to Chaplin's Cinema to listen to Kirsty Brook's presentation on the Panama Canal which we were due to transit the following day.

One look at her slides convinced me I was in for an experience I will never forget so I decided to avoid any risk of getting sunstroke and missing it all.

I had asked the comedian Peter Goodwright if I could talk to him about his career and he told me to meet him in Andersons Bar at 11.30am. Just as he came in there was dead silence on the ship.

"We've stopped," Peter said. "Any minute now there'll be a bing-bong and we'll get This is the Captain – you may have noticed we have stopped!"

Peter Goodwright

His imitation of Mike Carr was spot on and when the announcement came five minutes later we fell about laughing. Our stoppage was connected with Oriana's previous problem but two engineers had come on board at Curacao and were working on it.

It was not long before the air conditioning came on again and the ship started moving, first on half-power then picking up speed.

Peter told me he his first radio broadcast was in 1958 but he had been working the clubs before that.

"There is no nicer noise than a whole lot of people laughing, it is the goal you strive for but looking around for stories is not easy," he said.

"Sometimes I am jealous of singers who can sing a song whether anyone likes it or not. We have to make people laugh or we die a death."

Peter's first broadcast was in a talent competition, "What Makes a Star?". Winning that heat he went through to the next broadcast, "Second Chance," and finally "Third Time Lucky," which was when an agent heard him and took him on.

"It was all done in the Northern region," he said. "That is the honing ground for comedians. If you can make them laugh in Northern clubs you can make them laugh anywhere."

His first week in a variety show was in Chester but although he enjoys performing on stage he just loves the radio.

"I started off as an impressionist and you can sound like

someone but don't necessarily look like them," he said.

"Radio allowed me to be anything to anyone because they couldn't see me."

Peter's life has gone in stages, starting off as a variety artist. "The world which I knew has now completely and utterly disappeared," he said.

"There are now no landladies, no audiences and no theatres. In the old days the only place you could see your favourite artist was in the theatre but television, CDs and videos have changed all that."

He also feels the short pantomime runs have got people out of the habit of going to the theatre.

"Pantomimes used to run for months, not weeks as they do now," he said. "If you had a pantomime and a summer season that was your year mapped out, radio and television were the cream on the cake."

After variety came the clubs and when gambling came in the clubs got bigger but they faded out and radio came in.

"All my shows on radio were very successful," he said "I did The Peter Goodwright Show and then The Impressionists."

When television arrived Peter was on the show "Who Do You Do," for several years, but he said now television has completely changed.

"It's all how to put up guttering and programmes where they make people cry because they paint their bedrooms bright pink," he said.

He was glad his fellow comic Joe Pasquale won "I'm a Celebrity, Get Me Out of Here," but he would never do it even if he was asked.

"I'm too old for it and I enjoy my life too much to go through all that," he said.

When he was told television couldn't do variety any more because it was too expensive to pay the bands he wondered what he was going to do.

"Then I was offered a job as an after-dinner speaker and I enjoyed that," he said. "It's true that when one door shuts another opens but even that is now ruled by economic factors.

"The big companies hold board meetings to decide "Are we going to have Peter Goodwright or a fish course?

"So when that ended I thought, what now? Then cruising came in."

Peter loves cruising as he can bring his wife Norma with him and he said it is a wonderful opportunity to do shows.

He does five or six cruises a year, mostly for P & O, and when he flies back from San Francisco he plans to spend some time at home before the next one.

Home is between Shanklin and Ventnor on the Isle of Wight, high on a hill with beautiful views.

"This cruise came at just the right time," he said. "We have had builders in for ten months so we were glad to get away."

He has no plans to retire and as each stage of his life comes to a close he looks forward to the next one.

"Sooner of later the cruising will come to an end and then I will say "What's next.?"

Even stars of radio and TV have their heroes and Peter's are Laurel and Hardy.

"Their last ever performance was on stage at the Palace Theatre in Plymouth," he said. "Oliver Hardy was taken ill there and they returned to America where he had a dehabilitating stroke.

"When I played a week in Variety at the Palace Theatre I found it very exciting to be standing on the very spot where my heroes had stood."

As Peter left to find his wife for lunch and I got ready for Aquatic Sports and the greasy pole I thought how lucky we were to have such a real "showbiz old trouper" on board. It did not surprise me that the Theatre Royal was packed out for all his shows.

DAY THIRTEEN
THE PANAMA CANAL

There are certain days in your life that you know will stay with you forever and January 19th 2005 is certainly one of them.

Thirteen has always been lucky for me and the thirteenth day of my trip round the world could not have been luckier. It was the day I was to make my first transit down the Panama Canal and what a wonderful day it turned out to be.

I was up at 6.30am as I didn't want to miss anything. It was far too early as the pilot, due to be picked up at 7.20am did not come on board until 8.15am but there was so much to see.

Ships were lined up to go through the Port of Cristobal heading for the Gatun Locks which would take us into the famous Panama Canal. Normally there were two locks operating side by side but they were doing maintenance on the East Lock so all the ships had to go through the West Lock which resulted in quite a traffic jam.

Amanda Wilkins

The Panama Canal

Ahead of us was a cruise liner The Spirit of the Seas and round us were various tankers. The Panama Canal is approximately 80 kilometers (48 miles) and the triple Gatun Locks were the first of three we had to go through before we passed under the Bridge of the Americas and out into the Pacific Ocean.

At the first lock we had to be raised 26 meters above sea level to take us into Gatun Lake. To either side of us was lush greenery and we spotted some crocodiles at sea and on the sandbank.

It was here we crossed the Continental Divide, only to be lowered back to sea level on the opposite side of the Isthmus. Approximately 197million litres of fresh water are used for each lockage and ultimately flushed into the sea.

It costs Oriana £156,000 each time she transits the Panama Canal so she gets priority over most of the other shipping.

It took us about an hour to get through the locks into Gatun Lake and most people left the crowded decks after that to seek some shade as the temperature rose to 92 degrees. We had a few showers of rain, but they were welcome in the scorching heat.

The Panama Canal

I decided to get some shade at midday and enjoy the deck barbecue only to return to the open deck around 2pm.

By then we were in a narrow Gaillard or Culebra Cut with dense jungle to either side

This 12.6 stretch is the narrowest part of the Panama Canal and represents 15 per cent of its total length.

Everything was quiet except for the sound of some exotic birds in the trees and the gentle lapping of the water on the bow of the ship and I was overwhelmed by a feeling of tranquility and utter peace.

As we approached the Pedro Miguel Locks everything changed. The banks became industrial again and the loud hooter of the commuter train from Panama City to Cristobal could clearly be heard.

Then we saw the bright orange express, hooter blaring, race along the tracks in the distance. A tanker was alongside us waiting for the adjacent lock and together the mules (tractors) pulled us through. There was barely two feet of space between the sides of the liner and the lock so one false move would have destroyed our paintwork.

We could see our last lock, the Miraflores ahead of us as the two were very close then we steamed past the port of Bilbao under the Bridge of the Americas and out into the Pacific Ocean.

We could clearly see the skyscrapers of Panama City on our port side and the expensive hotels lining the banks.

It had taken us about eight hours to transit the Panama

Canal and as everyone reluctantly left the decks to get ready for dinner we all remarked what a great day it had been.

The experience has left a mark on my soul that will live with me forever and the peace I felt that day is something I will never forget.

DAY FOURTEEN
Poetry in Motion

After what seemed like months at sea we eventually clocked up 14 days since we sailed from Southampton.

Feeling slightly jaded from the hottest transit of the Panama Canal the Captain has ever known I decided to have a lazy day in the shade.

He said at one point the temperature had reached the mid-nineties and even in the shade it was 84 degrees so it was not surprising we were all roasting as we watched the rain forests glide by.

At 11am on day fourteen Cruise Director Christine Noble was chatting to Pam Ayres about her life and career in the Pacific Lounge.

I was glad I got there early as the large room quickly filled up. Pam arrived and said she was amazed so many people had chosen her above the sun.

She told how she was born in the small village of Stanford-in-the-Vale. "It used to be in Berkshire until they fiddled about with the boundaries and now we are in Oxfordshire," she said.

"We are very irritated about that because we liked being in Berkshire and if I am asked where I come from I always say North Berkshire."

She explained she gets irritated when people ask if she has to work on her accent. "Everyone in our village talked like that and I didn't realize I had an accent until I left home," she said.

She ran through her early life when she went to the village primary school which she left when she failed her 11 plus. She continued her education at Farringdon Secondary Modern School.

"It was quite sad really as the grammar school kids who passed their 11 plus waited for the bus one side of the road whilst us dismal failures waited on the other side," she said.

She blames her failure on her teacher and the local vicar. "On the day I failed he came in and talked to the teacher who was invigilating," she said. "They talked all through the exam and it distracted me so I have always blamed them."

Pam left school at 15 and her first job was as a clerical assistant for the Civil Service.

"I was at the exotic Didcot Depot which served the needs

of the army," she said. "If they wanted blankets they would order a pair and if they wanted nuts they would order a gross. Each order had a code and it was my job to fill in the correct code, day after day..

"It was absolutely riveting and one day I saw an advertisement for the RAF. There was this girl in uniform standing in a semi-circle of lovely pilots who were all looking at her with undisguised lust."

Pam went to Reading to join up and she said she would like to get her hands on the recruiting officer as she felt she was misled. "I am still looking for that pilot," she said.

She was in the RAF for four years and the service took her to Singapore, Germany and Cyprus.

She said serving in Singapore in 1966/67 really launched her career. "There was a very good theatre club and I appeared in one or two plays and people laughed which I liked.

"On Friday nights people got up and did their bit. I couldn't find anything written by anyone else I wanted to perform so I started to write my own."

She left the RAF with some GCEs she had passed and went on to do a shorthand/typing course which resulted in her getting a job at Morris' radiators in Oxford.

At the same time she started going to folk clubs and reciting her poems. Gradually she was invited to talk to women's institutes and she was paid £12 for one appearance, half her weekly wage.

She moved to Smiths Industries to be assistant to a Mr Skinner. "He never remembered my name and always came in and said Hello Gorgeous, and I was never really much cop," she said.

Whilst she was there she did a charity show and her act went so well she was invited to audition for Opportunity Knocks.

On her form she put writer and reciter of humourous verse and she was invited to audition almost immediately

"In those days the waiting list for a singer to audition was five years," she said "So I think it was quite a relief for them to find an unusual act. Keith Beckett, the producer, came up to me after my audition and asked who wrote my stuff."

Pam Ayres appeared on Opportunity Knocks hosted by Hughie Green in 1975 and won it. In 1976 she handed in her notice at Smiths Industries to try and make a go of her career."

"Mr Skinner heaved a sigh of relief and gave me a road atlas which was already out of date when he gave it to me," she said.

A question and answer session followed her talk and she was asked if she had ever considered writing a poem about P & O launderettes.

"No I always avoid violence and aggression," she said. "When I've poked my nose in there it does seem to be a place where you take your life in your hands, especially if you dare to touch someone else's washing!"

This year Pam celebrates 30 years in show business and travels all over the world. The huge round of applause she got from the passengers proved she is as popular now as she was in the seventies.

After a seafood buffet in the Oriental Restaurant it was out into the sunshine to top up my tan before preparing for the formal night ahead.

The black and white ball provoked many different combinations of the colours and passengers were spoilt for choice for entertainment.

Peter Goodwright was making his last cabaret appearance before leaving the ship in San Francisco. The John James Trio was playing for the Black and White Ball and the popular band Powerhouse was paying tribute to all our favourite jazz legends.

It was very much a case of dipping in and out of three different venues to make sure you didn't miss anything but Peter Goodwright was so funny I watched his hour-long show before moving on to the next entertainment hub..

DAY FIFTEEN
Fun Friday

It is strange that after fourteen days at sea I was still discovering entertainments I had missed.

Coming out of the Cyb@study I heard the musical quiz being announced in the Crow's Nest bar. It had been running at 12.15 pm every sea day since Southampton but I had missed it in my Good Morning sheet.

Pianist Martin Green played extracts from 20 tunes and we were told the answers all contained the name of a place but he needed the full title of the tune.

The Yellow Rose of Texas was quickly followed by Are You Going to Scarborough Fair and I thought how easy it was. That was my downfall, after that I could not answer a single question.

I have several CDs of The Carpenters' songs as they were a firm favourite of mine but although I recognized On Top of The World I could not remember the words!

I have seen Evita many times but when Martin played Don't Cry for Me Argentina my mind went a complete blank. I knew it was from Evita and it was when Eva Peron made her impassioned speech from the Calla Rosa balcony in Argentina so why wouldn't the title come?

The winning lady got twenty out of twenty and richly deserved her bottle of champagne.

It was all good fun and something I intended to do again.

This was very much a day to relax and have fun and the chef had served up a sumptuous Mexican buffet in the Oriental restaurant with the best chilli con carne I have ever tasted.

After lunch I discovered how seriously the seasoned cruisers take their deck competitions. I reached my fourth shuffleboard final as I had an excellent partner. We were neck and neck with out opponents until the last chuck was sent down the court and we won by seven points.

Shaking hands with our opponents I gratefully accepted my long-awaited prize only to hear a voice behind me saying we had not won.

I turned round and saw our red-faced male opponent angrily addressing the harassed entertainment officer.

"We've only played five ends," he said. "We should have played six." A quick calculation found he was right and my partner and I handed back our prizes and resumed our positions on the court.

My partner had to battle it out with the female half of our opposing team. With one more chuck to come down the court we were still ahead, then disaster struck. My partner's chuck landed in the minus 10 box and it was all over, I had lost my fourth final.

Graciously we congratulated our opponents and they were handed their prizes, P & O notepads.

"I don't want this," the man said. "I won one of these playing whist."

A new innovation on day 15 was the tap class run by Elaine, one of the entertainment staff who is a former dancer.

When Devonshire Park Theatre in Eastbourne staged Stepping Out for the summer season a few years ago one of the company ran tap workshops on Saturday mornings. I had gone along and found that I thoroughly enjoyed it.

Not expecting to find these classes on Oriana I had not brought my tap shoes but I wore some court shoes with a small heel.

Elaine taught us a basic routine step by step and at the end of the 45 minute class we all managed to perform it in a fashion. Perhaps not up to professional standard yet but who knows what we will have achieved by the end of the 80 day trip.

The fun continued into the evening with Oriana's very own version of The Weakest Link.

With the name changed to Don't Break The Chain entertainment officer Gary Morris gave an excellent impression of Anne Robinson.

Among his/her victims were Pam Ayres and special interest lecturer Mike Harvey who got into the spirit of the show.

It was one of the funniest evenings we have had on the ship and the head-to-head was between Pam Ayres and the Captain's wife Angie Carr. When Pam went home with two bottles of wine and Angie went home with nothing there was a cheer that nearly took the roof of the room off.

As we were nearing the end of the first leg of the cruise, which is the end of the holiday for several passengers getting off at San Francisco, Oriana staged its first late-night cabaret since leaving Southampton.

Just before midnight singer Julie A'Scott performed a special tribute to Barbara Streisand in the Crow's Nest bar.

Even though we were in port in Acapulco the following day she had a good audience who appreciated her great voice and it was a fitting end to an action-packed fun day at sea.

DAY SIXTEEN
Going Loco in ACAPULCO

Our late arrival in Acapulco due to Oriana's technical problems and the work on the locks in the Panama Canal left me with a dilemma.

I had booked on an early morning tour to see the world famous cliff divers (clavadistas) for which Acapulco is famous.. They have been diving off the rocks at La Quebrada since 1934 and they plunge past the jagged rocks into a small crevice.

My tour was scheduled to leave the ship at 8.30am but as we did not dock until 10.30am it had been rescheduled for noon arriving back at the ship at 4pm. This would have left me no time to see the real Acapulco as the tour also visited several smart hotels and drove round the bay.

I therefore decided to leave the divers for another day and explore the town on foot. I was wary about going on my own so when an official tourist guide called Leonardo (after Leonardo de Caprio) offered to take me to the flea market El Parazal I decided I was safe.

Behind me were several other passengers and two of them, Dennis and Vicky, had obviously decided to keep an eye on me. When we left the sea front and started to go up the back streets I looked round and they were only too happy to join me. We went into the heart of old Acapulco which is far removed from the millionaire's playground at the other side of the bay.

Here it is a dirty Mexican town where the drivers constantly use their horns and expect pedestrians to get out of their way. You take your life in your hands every time you cross a road, even on a red light.

Leo took us further and further away from the ship into narrow, smelly streets and Dennis said it was time to turn back. But Leo insisted we were nearly there and turned quite nasty when he was told we would rather be on our own. He said he wanted to take us to "his brother's shop", which is what all the guides were telling the passengers.

He pointed out the entrance to the market and angrily left us to our own devices, grumbling because he had not received a large tip. The market was very dark and forbidding and Vicky said she felt uncomfortable going in there, as I did. But we ventured down the narrow lanes, stopping to bargain for some Mexican silver before emerging once again into the bright sunlight.

This time Dennis guided us back to the seafront and we decided to walk round the bay. I was amazed at the contrast between the old and the new. Here were the long sandy beaches with colourful umbrellas that made the resort so fashionable with the rich and famous.

The author meets the local police in Acapulco

Perched high on a hill was the house owned by John Wayne where he used to sit and throw his beer bottles on to the rocks below. The majestic coastal hills of the Sierra Madre plunge down almost into the city which stretches along the bay.

The hey-day for Acapulco was the 1940s when celebrities like Errol Flynn and Lana Turner owned homes there.

Although the "beautiful people" have long gone, the Western side of the bay boasts luxury hotels like the Hyatt Regency and the Acapulco Princess.

Back to the terminal where I stopped at the bar for a Marguarita cocktail that nearly blew your head off I boarded Oriana to have lunch and get some respite from the sun.

In the afternoon I decided to go the other way and visit the Cathedral of Nuestra Senora de la Soledad.

Standing on the Zocalo (main square) this peculiar Byzantine-style building with its bulbous domes looks more like something out of a film set than the House of God.

Walking the four or so blocks to the square I encountered the real misery of Mexico. Children as young as four and five were begging in the streets, coming up with boxes of sweets asking us to buy, while their mothers sat at the roadside watching them. I gave one little girl a dollar to take her photograph but you can't give to them all and it was heartbreaking to see their little faces screwed up with disappointment.

Opposite our berth was the El Fuerte de San Diego. The fort has a floor plan shaped like a star and when it was originally built in the 18th century pirates, many of them English, began raiding Acapulco for the treasure flowing through the town. The main export was silver, which Mexico is famous for.

The Spaniards decided to erect proper defences on a small hill overlooking the port but these were destroyed by an earthquake and were rebuilt in 1784. The Fort now houses the Museo Historico de Acapulco.

I was sorry not to have seen the divers but very glad I had seen the real Acapulco, not just the beautiful side of the town seen by the passengers who chose to go on the excursions.

Despite a hot tiring day everyone rallied round in the evening for a Hoedown at the Cruise Director's Country and Western Night.

For those passengers doing the First Leg of the World Cruise there was only a few more days to go. I had another 65 days and several more new and exciting ports to look forward to.

DAY SEVENTEEN
Tears and Laughter.

After line dancing under the stars on the open deck until midnight the previous day there was a lethargic atmosphere around the ship on day seventeen.

I joined several other passengers for the port lecture on San Francisco before attending the church service.

Throughout the cruise the chefs have been coming up with some excellent ideas to make sure we put on as much weight as possible and this was the day of the Indian buffet lunch in the Oriental Restaurant.

After eating a fine selection of curries I certainly did not feel like rushing around playing deck games in the afternoon and I decided to go to the cinema for the first time since we sailed from Southampton.

It was the last showing of the superb film starring Jude Law, Nicole Kidman and Renee Zellweger, Cold Mountain.

I have the video but I had never seen it on the large screen with stereo sound and it was even better than when I had watched it at home.

There were not many dry eyes in Chaplin's Cinema when the very sad ending came and I was glad I had decided to see it instead of playing shuffleboard.

We had been told that as we neared San Francisco the temperatures would drop and there was a distinct change in the weather.. Still wearing shorts I was told by the Staff Captain that I would need a sweater, trousers and a waterproof in two day's time when I visited my first American city.

But luckily it was only to be a brief lull as I knew we would be back in the warm weather as we got closer to Hawaii.

The packed entertainment programme in the evening had been so well arranged that we could go to everything.

Getting out of dinner a bit early I headed for All the Fun of the Fair, a Charity Night in aid of Seamen's Charities..

For the first time we were allowed to buy chips with cash instead of using our cruise card to sign our life away. I was finding this very dangerous as you don't realize how much your bill is totting up as you order yet another "Cocktail of the Day."

Luckily we could settle our bills at the end of each leg, but it was still a worry that my on board credit would not last the full 80 days!

Chips were only 20p each so I bought £10 worth as it was for such a good cause. There was an excellent tombola where I came away armed with assorted prizes and headed for the gambling tables.

I won money on the card race and another card game of skill but it was on the putting green I really excelled myself.

I scored nothing at my first attempt having failed to putt a single ball through the target hole and one at my second attempt. I fared little better at the darts but it was all good fun and my golfing prowess prompted a crowd of laughing onlookers.

The theatre company presented Follies fifteen minutes later than usual and what a superb show it was. The costumes were worthy of any West End stage.

Finally I went to the Casino to enter the roulette tournament but failed to make the final. The idea was to purchase chips for £5 and bet as heavily as possible for five spins so the top seven scorers went into a grand final to win £100. It was the only night when I could pile up chips on any part of the cloth at random because I knew I wasn't losing real money.

DAY EIGHTEEN
Hail and Farewell

You cannot come on board Oriana
without having Breakfast at Tiffanys.

The wood panelled bar with the beautiful stained glass ceiling serves up continental breakfast every morning which comprises bagels with smoked salmon and cream cheese accompanied by filter coffee.

There are other choices as well but that is what Janet and I opted for and there was no charge for choosing this venue above others to start off your day

I knew from the moment I met Janet I had struck gold. A widow in her seventies on her first World Cruise she has a tremendous sense of humour and we got on very well from day one.

After breakfast I decided to venture into the danger zone on Oriana, the launderette. There are several on various decks and the nearest one to me was one deck above.

Remembering Pam Ayres' words it was with some trepidation I ventured in and I was amazed to hear the sound of laughter. Faced with an industrial machine I had never seen before I had to ask a gentleman to show me how to use it and that prompted more laughter.

The launderettes are the centre for all the gossip on the ship and I was told an extraordinary story that I have no proof is true. But as one lady passenger told me it had happened on a previous cruise she had done and I heard it from two separate sources I can only think it is.

In one of the launderettes on board a fight ensued between a male and female passenger. She had gone off and left her washing in the dryer and as the man wanted to use it he took it out and put his in..

Coming back to discover what he had done she slapped his face and he promptly slapped her back. The story goes that they were both put off the ship in Acapulco and told to make their own way home.

After I had done my domestic chores I paid my second visit to the cinema in two days. On the recommendation of many passengers I decided to go to the final showing of De-Lovely, the bio-pic about composer Cole Porter.

I was so pleased I had made that decision as it was such a

good film and I revelled in nostalgia as I listened to his songs I knew so well.

The temperature in the afternoon dropped to 69 degrees, a marked contrast to the 80 degrees plus we had become used to. With San Francisco fast approaching we all knew the weather was getting colder and would stay like that for the next few days.

Sweaters I had pushed into my suitcase under my bed had to be pulled out and I had to search the wardrobe for my thick trousers and abandon my shorts.

If we were lucky we would have one more day of sunbathing before we reached the American city.

Pam Ayres was due to give her last show of the cruise but as I had seen her twice I decided to dance the night away.

It is strange doing a World Cruise which is divided into five legs. The penultimate night before San Francisco where we were due to lose several passengers and gain more we attended the Farewell Ball for those that were departing the ship.

There was a tinge of sadness for those getting off and for those of us on board who were losing newly made friends. But there was also the anticipation of meeting new people who would be coming on board in America to travel with us to Australia and beyond

DAY NINETEEN
Celebrations

On the nineteenth day of the first month of 2005 it was a day of celebration on board Oriana.

There was a lunchtime Australian Get-Together in the Lords Tavern with music by the John James Trio. This was to celebrate Australia Day on January 26, the day we were due to arrive in San Francisco.

It was also Burns Night and everyone on board who possessed a drop of Scottish blood was looking forward to the evening celebrations.

The weather drastically deteriorated with the temperature dropping to 59 degrees and only the most hardy remained on the decks. For the first time since the beginning of the cruise the Riviera Bar by the swimming pool was closed and Janet and I deserted the open deck for breakfast and opted for the restaurant instead.

An extra bingo session was held in the morning with a

crowd of passengers vying with each other to win the jackpot which had reached a massive £1,650. As this was the last day of the first leg of the cruise it had to be won. At the morning session the winner had to get a full house in 58 numbers and disappointment reverberated round the room when it was not won.

This meant that the money would go to the first person getting a full house at the afternoon session so a large queue formed as people lined up to buy tickets.

Having lost £10 trying to win the jackpot in the morning I decided my chances of getting it were very slim and I gave the afternoon session a miss in favour of my tap dancing. In the end there were two winners who shared £825 each.

This cruise was proving to be one of the most eventful voyages I had ever taken. At 12 noon the officer of the watch said Oriana was being surveyed by an American plane that was flying round and round above the ship.

Shortly afterwards Captain Mike Carr came on the loudspeaker to tell us that he had been asked by the US Naval Patrol Fleet to alter course.

This was due to an exercise where they were firing missiles and Oriana had to change direction by 120 degrees and zig zag across the ocean until the Captain was told otherwise.

At 1:05 pm he was allowed to resume his north westerly course for San Francisco. We were warned the weather forecast in the city was not good, mist, rain and a temperature of about 50 degrees, very similar to the UK. This would be a big shock to the system after the searing temperatures we had become used to.

Due to the position of the ship and the low cloud Oriana was out of touch with the satellite which provided passengers with phone calls and emails. As several of them were due to leave the ship the following day there was a lot of frustration that people could not phone or email from the ship. Communication for all of us was virtually cut off.

For the first time I decided to watch an in-house video on the television in my cabin and I was delighted with the range of films on offer. For three hours I lay on my bed watching Robert Redford in The Horse Whisperer, followed by Chicago which inspired me for my tap dancing class.

Dinner was very special that night as they piped in the haggis at both sittings. The entertainment again was plentiful with a top of the bill variety show featuring all the artists on the first leg. There was also a talent show presented by the passengers which featured the line dancers. Those of us doing tap dancing were warned we would be required to appear in the show at the end of the second leg.

Having Scottish blood in my ancestry I opted to attend the Burns Night Celebration with the splendid band Powerhouse. At 10.30pm they turned it over to a Ceilidh and we all had a "reel" good time.

DAY TWENTY
I left my heart in SAN FRANCISCO

There are few places in the world where you can be yourself and revert to childhood if you so wish.

San Francisco is one of them. It established itself in the sixties when the hippies congregated in the Haight-Ashbury district. Everyone of my generation played Scott Walker's record, If you are going to San Francisco be sure to wear flowers in your hair.

Ever since then I have longed to visit the city and so on the twentieth day of my mammoth voyage I got up at 4.30am to get my first glimpse of an American skyscraper.

It was cold and wet, pouring with rain in fact, but there were plenty of people as mad as me who were determined to see us go under the famous Golden Gate Bridge.

We did this at 5am but it was so dark we could not see much until we were right below it.

We had been warned the immigration officers might take

up to four hours to clear the ship but they were remarkably quick and I was ashore by 9.30am.

Walking along towards Pier 39 I decided to copy Judy Garland and hopped on a tram that took me to China Town. I was very tempted to sing Clang clang clang goes the trolley but decided to spare my fellow passengers.

The author riding the trolley in San Francisco

Chinatown houses the biggest Chinese community outside Asia and you enter it via the ornamental arch of dragons and lions. Once inside there is not a lot to see except a plethora of shops and restaurants.

Returning the way I came I made straight for the world-famous Fisherman's Wharf where San Francisco's fishing fleets have been unloading their catch since the 1940's. But it was further along the waterfront on Pier 39 the fun really began and that is where I spent most of the day.

This wooden-built complex is fast becoming a rival to Fisherman's Wharf, which was once San Francisco's premier attraction.

From the end of the pier I got an excellent view of Alcatraz Island, once the federal prison which housed convicts such as Al Capone, Robert "Birdman" Stroud and "Machine Gun" Kelly.

Alcatraz

It closed as a prison in 1963 and is now a tourist attraction with boat trips taking you out there from Pier 41. As the tour included locking you in a prison cell I decided against it for obvious reasons.

It was on K-Wharf on Pier 39 that I saw the most extraordinary sight. Playing happily or sleeping on several pontoons in the West Marina were hundreds of Californian sea lions. The noise they made was incredible and could clearly be heard from the deck of the ship as we approached the port.

The Pier 39 Sea Lions

They chose to make this their home following the 1989 San Francisco earthquake and the boisterous barking pinnipeds starting arriving in droves, taking over the dock completely in January 1990.

At first there were about 50 but due to a plentiful herring supply the number has grown to more than 300 and a multitude of visitors come from all over the world to see them. I spent more than an hour sitting on the wooden viewing platform watching their antics.

The rain stopped mid morning and the mist cleared to give fine views of Alcatraz, Telegraph Hill topped by the Colt Tower and the Golden Gate Bridge.

It was on Pier 39 that I reverted to my childhood starring in a video in the Flying Carpet Ride shop.

I sat cross-legged on a Turkish carpet on a green revolving platform. The girl making the video told me when to fall off the carpet, punch to the side and lie on my back with my legs in the air. The resulting video is hilarious, I am flying upside down over the Golden Gate Bridge, soaring like Superwoman over Alcatraz and my punches knock a cyclist off his bike. A great souvenir of a fun place and well worth the $40 I paid for the video and a colour photograph of my magic carpet ride.

Feeling like a kid again I came across another attraction from my youth – a beautifully painted carousel with more than a dozen horses going up and down to the music. Disappointed no-one was queuing up to ride on it the attendant told me he would operate it just for me. Sitting in solitude on one of the horses I caused much hilarity from fellow passengers walking past who stopped to watch.

No visit to San Francisco would be complete without buying a beer in the Hard Rock Café. The bartender, looking just like Tom Cruise in Cocktail, made me very welcome and asked me all about the ship whilst I sat surrounded by priceless memorabilia of the heady days of rock.

All too soon it was time to return to the ship but our American pie was not over yet. For an hour we were entertained on board by the Fog City Jazz Band, the premier San Francisco Dixieland and Swing Band. When the musicians were introduced to us it turned out several of them had played with the jazz greats of the past.

Of all the ports we had visited so far San Francisco had to be my favourite. Never mind the cold and the rain, this is a fun city and I hope one day I can return and spend more time there.

DAY TWENTY-ONE
Luck Be a Lady

Twenty-one days out of Southampton we woke up to grey skies, an equally grey and vicious sea and intermittent rain. There was a very large swell and once again the deck doors were taped off and a net was put over the swimming pools.

It was a day to be indoors and hang on to anything and everyone you could to avoid falling over. After the heat we had been used to this inclement spell came as a nasty shock.

After a morning reading in my cabin I decided to put myself in the hands of fate and try the slot machines.

I had played on odd occasions allowing myself £2 a time but on this horrible day I decided to splash out and change a fiver into 10p tokens.

Many people had the same idea and there was silence in the room except for the sound of the slot machines and the welcome sound of coins pouring into the tray when someone got lucky.

My £5 disappeared into thin air within an hour and I

moved on to the Casino. I changed another £5 into 25p chips and spent a pleasant hour at the roulette table. Luck was on my side this time and when I was £1 up I decided to quit while I was ahead.

Again the harassed cruise director Christine Noble had to alter the evening programme at very short notice.

With the ship rocking and rolling from the heavy swell it was too dangerous for the dancers in the planned show, There's No Business Like Show Business, to perform..

Several cabaret artists joined and the international singer song/writer Gerard Kenny agreed to stage his show one day early.

P & O certainly excelled themselves on this cruise with the standard of entertainment and Gerard made us all forget the miserable day we had spent on board A talented writer of hits such as New York, New York he also showed us what a great performer he is as well.

With the dining room vastly depleted due to the movement of the ship everyone went to bed hoping they would wake up to a bright new day.

DAY TWENTY TWO
Hurricanes Hardly Happen

In the early hours of the morning of the twenty second day we encountered the edge of a hurricane. We were en route from San Francisco to Honolulu and I had expected the weather to be like it was in the film South Pacific.

It was a shock to find we were moving around even more than we did in the days that followed Southampton.

One minute I was lying quietly in my bed, the next I felt I was being thrown up in the air and when I was facing towards Janet's bed I felt I was going to fall out any minute.

At no time did I experience fear as I knew Oriana was built to withstand the worst weather possible. But I found it difficult to sleep and I tossed and turned most of the night.

In the morning the swell was huge but there was the faint glimmer of weak sunshine and ever hopeful that the worst was over I dressed in my shorts and an Oriana sweatshirt and went to the top deck to play shuffleboard.

I was faced with a few fellow passengers wrapped up for an English winter and when I was asked to score the first game on the shady side of the ship I knew why. I have never been so cold in my life and I was very glad when my partner and I were knocked out in the first round.

I decided to seek out the warmer climes inside the ship and attended my first line dancing session. I found it great fun and thought I might even forego the sun to attend the classes regularly.

Many of us "all-rounders" were starting to worry the tans we had built up in the Panama Canal would soon disappear and when the Oriana grapevine said it would be raining in Honolulu all hopes of brighter weather ahead evaporated.

I sunk into a deep depression and when I am depressed I spend money! I decided I had to have the Frank Usher dress I had been looking at ever since the second week of the cruise. Reduced to £112 it was a pale yellow hand-made dress covered in sequins – just right for my second Captain's cocktail party of the cruise.

Taking two sizes back to my cabin to try on I was amazed after three weeks at sea I could get into a size 12 instead of my usual size 14 and I felt like Marilyn Monroe.

Dressed for the party I felt like the cat's whiskers as I went to show the girls in the shop."Amanda what are you doing?" they said. "You've got the dress on the wrong way round!"

Thinking it zipped up at the back Janet had poured me into it and although I thought the design was strange I assumed it was what Frank Usher had conceived.

One of the girls took me behind the racks of clothes and re-dressed me and I found I not only felt like Marilyn Monroe, but looked like her with a cleavage I had never had before.

This time I went in the right door and was photographed with the Captain after treading heavily on his toes as the ship gave a lurch.

A lot of time is spent in the restaurant when you are on the cruise and getting the table right is very important. On the first leg we had a very good table where we all gelled and Charlie (I never knew his other name) kept us in stitches with his tales of his previous cruises and his passion for horse racing.

Sadly he left us at San Francisco, along with another lady so we were left with three empty spaces. My other two table companions had become romantically involved and often dined under the stars in Le Jardin Bistro so I was hoping we would have a full table.

But only one mature gentleman joined us. He was a complete contrast to Charlie who had a great sense of humour.and told me he didn't really want to be there, he wanted a table on his own!

On the night we sailed from San Francisco it was just the two of us at the table and we both found it hard going. After dinner on day 22 I was even more depressed as I did not want to become one of P & O's habitual complainers.

I was saved from my attack of the blues by an old friend of mine, Nigel Phillips, who was P & O's Bar Manager. He came on board the ship at San Francisco to work the rest of the cruise. In retrospect after the cruise was over I realized this was the worst thing that could have happened.

One of the bravest men I know having suffered from cancer of the tongue he has now made a complete recovery and is back to working to his full capacity. I had been warned that being at sea for so long would bring good and bad days but Nigel's calming influence quickly restored my equilibrium and made me realize what a lot of good things lay ahead in the days to come. I had not seem him for six years and I found him as charming and good looking as ever and I was looking forward to spending time with him during the two months we were to sail the seas together.

DAY TWENTY-THREE
Singing the Blues

On the twenty-third day out from Southampton the ship was like a morgue. There was an atmosphere of gloom everywhere you went.

Disconsolate passengers sat around the foyers on any chair they could find desperate for something to do. The entertainment staff had laid on a programme of activities as usual but the majority of the people had been hit by an attack of the blues and they just did not want to join in.

Outside the wind was howling, the sea was grey and the decks on the starboard side were wet with spray.

One man said he thought once we got past San Francisco into the Pacific it would all be sunshine and light. The passengers who joined at Southampton were experiencing a real case of déjà vu and worrying about losing their tans.

Those who joined at San Francisco were beginning to think they would never see the sun. My blues, lifted by Nigel on the previous night, had returned with the depressing outlook.

My spirits lifted when I attended line dancing for an hour before lunch but plummeted again when I lost £10 on blackjack in the casino for want of something to do.

Having sworn not to go to bingo this leg of the cruise after spending £5 a day in the first three weeks I told my cabin-mate I thought it was the only alternative. She said she would come with me and as a virgin player she immediately won £40 – I went away with nothing!

The evening brought a promise of better things. The restaurant manager moved me to a table for six. There was a Canadian, Edward Hunter and his American travelling companion Carol Bartol, a couple who had joined at San Francisco and another lady who also changed her table because she was unhappy like me.

Immediately I knew it was a good move. Conversation flowed on every subject under the sun, including opening a book on how many people would die on the World Cruise. Apparently this is the norm as the average age of the passengers doing the round trip is quite high.

Our table was by the window in the restaurant and the noise from the sea was incredible. It was on the same deck as our cabin which is just above water level, so the huge waves would crash against the window.

The movement of the ship subsided enough in the evening to enable the theatre company to stage another brilliant show. This time the choice was There's No Business Like Show Business with the artists making several very quick changes from the boxes strategically placed round the stage.

The show brought cheers and whistles from the audience as their spirits soared with the fast moving show.

In the Lords Tavern a number of passengers showed their prowess on the karaoke machine and the atmosphere around the decks of Oriana boded well as people once again got into a party mood.

DAY TWENTY-FOUR
The Swinging Sixties

What a difference a day makes.

On the 24th day of my journey I woke up to sunshine.

Passengers starved of warmth hurried to reserve their sunbeds before anyone else could get there.

Bikinis were the dress of the day and a barbecue was set up on deck by the pool in preparation for a very welcome lunch in the open air.

The wind was still very strong which made playing shuffleboard or quoits almost impossible and the swell had not abated so people were still staggering around the ship. But the difference was they were smiling and the gloomy atmosphere that had existed on the ship the previous day had completely disappeared.

I went to the church service and for the first time since we left Southampton we did not have For Those In Peril on the Sea.

On a Sunday all activities are re-scheduled to allow passengers time to attend the service and it is a mad rush after the National Anthem to get to where you are supposed to be.

Hurrying to get to line dancing the ship lurched and I felt my back twist. A few years previously I had slipped a disc in the upper part of my spine and I was warned to take extra care if I suffered back pain again.

It was not that painful and as the medical charges on the ship are very high I decided to carry on as normal and hope it would go away.

I managed one line dance but the grapevine (putting my left foot behind my right) put a strain on my back and the pain started again so I dropped out.

Resting it for the day I thought I would chance tap dancing as we were told we were due to put on a show at the end of this leg of the cruise but 30 minutes was enough.

With my back as stiff as a board I went to the beauty salon and asked about a massage. They immediately gave me an appointment and told me to get some heat on my back first in the sauna.

Then Gemma went to work. With hands as soft as a butterfly she smoothed out the tension and I came out 30 minutes later feeling thoroughly refreshed and with no aches and pains.

It was sixties/seventies night on the ship and the Oriana Theatre Company, which had built up a huge following, staged Gold Discs and Platform Shoes.

For the first time, apart from Aladdin, the production had a story. It showed a middle-aged couple reminiscing about the happy times at the local disco in the sixtees and seventies.

They took part in an all-important dance contest but failed to win, so thirty years later they decide to have a reunion at the same venue – The Inferno – and re-stage the dance contest to see if this time they could go home with the elusive trophy.

The result was hilarious and full of nostalgia for us "oldies" who lived through the golden era of The Beatles, The Village People, Grease and platform shoes.

I recognized clothes and white pvc boots I had worn so proudly and the front row in the Theatre Royal all joined in the actions for YMCA.

The audience would not let the company go and cheered and whistled for more – the first time they had done an encore of any show.

When sadly they finally brought down the curtain the evening was not over. It was into Harlequins to dance the night away to sixties music performed by Powerhouse.

The moans and complaints of the long days at sea in bad weather since San Francisco were forgotten as the passengers let down their hair and lost their inhibitions as they all pretended to be teenagers again dancing at the local disco.

With the clocks going back another hour, to make us ten hours behind the UK, no-one was worried about the early start in Honolulu the following day.

DAY TWENTY FIVE
Aloha Aloha. HAWAII

Life is nought but a series of disappointments. I wrote that in my teenage days when I used to religiously keep a five year diary. I must have suffered some terrible crisis although I have no recollection of it now.

I had a pre-conceived idea of Hawaii – sun-kissed beaches of golden sand, surfers riding huge waves, hula girls in their grass skirts and palm trees. I had faithfully watched every episode of Hawaiian Five-O and seen Elvis gyrating his hips in Blue Hawaii.

Drawing back the curtains as we drew into the island's capital Honolulu I could not believe my eyes. We were shrouded in mist and I could spot drizzle.

Dressing to see us come alongside I was faced with masses of concrete skyscrapers and a cold, dismal morning. A choir was singing Hawaiian music to welcome us in but they looked incongruous in the back of a tent to keep the rain off them.

I also expected to step off the gangway and be presented

with a floral lei by a grass-skirted maiden as in the old films, but all we got was a security guard showing us into a long concrete tunnel where we were sniffed by the beagles to make sure we had brought nothing edible ashore.

Out into the streets I went to the Aloha shopping mall to have a look round and bought an artificial lei for six dollars. It was very pretty, but not quite the same. I bought an Elvis-type ukulele for the Newhaven and Seaford Sea Cadets who were plotting my trip as part of a project.

I decided to go up the Aloha Tower, the Liberty Statue of Honolulu, at the South end of Fort Street on Pier 9.

From the top you can get a panoramic view from Pearl Harbour to Diamond Head. But a squat security guard refused me entry. I tried to explain I could not take the tiny tin elevator up 10 floors as I was claustrophobic and asked if I could use the stairs, but he would not budge and said no member of the public could use them.

Walking to the post office to send a package home was quite an experience. I had to cross four major roads and jaywalking is an offence with a heavy fine. You press a button then wait for what seems a very long time for the little green man to permit you to cross.

I was told by Angie Carr, the Captain's wife that I must not judge Hawaii on Honolulu so I took a taxi round part of the island. First stop was the world-famous Waikiki Beach, three-and-a-half miles south-east of the downtown area.

The traffic was very heavy and it took us longer than it should to get there. My taxi driver said he would wait while I walked on the beach and took some photographs. Still the sun did not shine and the golden sand I had expected looked black as it was interspersed with grit. It was very crowded and although the beach was piled high with surfboards there were no surfers riding massive waves.

The security guard in the booth told me Waikiki used to be one of the greatest beaches in the world but it was now run-down as I found out.

We passed several green parks and went into the mountains, the top of which were shrouded in mist. We should have had a spectacular view down to the bay but the heavy cloud prevented us from getting the full benefit.

The scenery was very beautiful but much the same as I saw during our transit of the Panama Canal.

Back to the terminal I had a last walk round the Aloha Centre and had my photograph taken with a group of parrots. Two on my arms, two on my shoulder and one on my head! The one on my left shoulder was fascinated by my emerald earring and continually pecked it. I had visions of my treasured precious stone disappearing down its gullet.

Four television actors joined the ship in Honolulu to present two straight plays. Fraser Hines, better known as Joe Sugden from Emmerdale, Susan Hodge and Vicki Michelle from Allo Allo and Robert Duncan who played Gus in Drop The Dead Donkey.

They were due to perform two comedies between Honolulu and Hong Kong and would go into rehearsal the day after Hawaii.

I was shopping when I bumped into Fraser and Vicki. I didn't recognize her at first but I recognized Fraser as I had reviewed him and Robert in "Outside Edge" for the Brighton Argus. "Do you remember me?" I asked and he beamed. "Of course I do, we met in Eastbourne and you fancied the pants off Robert. You know he is on board?"

As we sailed past the Diamond Head Crater at the end of Waikiki Beach I felt no regrets at leaving Hawaii as I did when we sailed from our previous ports of call.

I found my opinion of Hawaii was shared by a number of passengers who had also had preconceived ideas.

This was the only port of call where I was expecting what I did not get and I realized as we left it was hopefully the only one where I would be disappointed.

The evening's entertainment gave us the second round of Don't Break the Chain with Gary Morris repeating his Anne Robinson impersonation.

This time the contestants were made up of the Oriana Theatre Company who were not so well known to the passengers as the previous ones.

Although it was amusing it was not quite as funny as the final battle between Captain's wife Angie Carr and Pam Ayres. Or maybe the blues that had hit me in Hawaii continued into the evening.

DAY TWENTY-SIX
Sing, Sing a Song

Sunshine was the order of the day and every sun lounger was occupied by an oiled body as soon as the sun was up.

I was on target for reaching the most shuffleboard finals and winning none of them.. With my competition on day 25 of the cruise my tally stood at five.

I thought I might join the cricketers in the afternoon but one look at the powerful bowling by the Australian passengers made me decide this was men's territory and I should stick to shuffleboard where I belonged.

After being in the sun all day I went back on my resolution of not playing bingo this leg of the cruise as it was costing me £5 a day. I got very excited when I needed just two numbers to win the snowball jackpot of £1,150 but sadly the 49 numbers went without the jackpot being won so it would now rise to £1,200.

I could not even win the £200 consolation prize as someone else pipped me to the post and I realized I was destined never to be a bingo winner on this cruise. By the end of the 80 days I would have financed a smart new ball machine for P & O!

It was time to don our best frocks for the Ladies Night Ball but suddenly I became a "cruise oldie" like all the other veteran travellers. I was comparing the ball with days gone by when it was run by the entertainment staff and it was fun.

Now, although they were in attendance, it was run by the dance instructors Tony and Lorraine. The programme included all the dances they taught in their class and I felt preference was given to their regulars.

After one dance with the deputy cruise director James I left for the casino where I promptly lost £15 on roulette.

Travelling solo is a lonely experience if you like dancing. You cannot go up to strangers and drag them away from their wives. When I mentioned this to cruise director Ian Fraser, who took over half way through from Christine he said. "Single people are a problem. The wives don't like them as they seem them as a threat.."

Luckily the acute loneliness I felt towards the end of the cruise had not hit me as I was still excited about the rest of the trip.

In the theatre the company had staged a further performance of Aladdin, although they had said the one on the last leg would be the final performance. I did not see it again but the four actors who came on at Honolulu attended and Frazer Hines said they all loved it.

The highlight of the evening was the midnight cabaret by international singer songwriter Gerard Kenny.

The Crow's Nest was transformed into a New York piano bar as Gerard went back to his roots singing for the passengers unaccompanied by the orchestra.

Despite the late hour Kenny's Piano Bar was packed and encore after encore was called for.

I had met Gerard on deck a few days before and when he heard my name was Amanda he said he would sing the Barry Manilow song Mandy for me.

He was as good as his word, calling out for me so he could see where I was and singing it especially for me. It was the first time an artist of his calibre had sung just for me and it is one of the milestones in my life that will be recorded for ever.

After the performance Gerard agreed to meet me the following day to talk about his life and career.

A number of passengers going all the way round had

started to niggle about the amount of time spent at sea between ports, but looking at our schedule before we sailed we knew there would be several passages of four or five days without seeing land. It was the longest sea voyage I had ever taken and they were days when I found I was doing the same thing day after day.

I never once felt I wanted to return home to a cold and frosty UK but after the bad weather we had gone through between San Francisco and Hawaii I found I couldn't wait to get off the ship again.

When the sun shone brilliantly as it did from the moment we left Honolulu it made things much easier and smiles returned to the faces of the passengers. But despite the vastness of Oriana after nearly four weeks of living in a false world where five course dinners were the norm I did find periods when I longed to return to normality.

Cash is never used on the P & O ships, everything is charged to your cruise card. So you sign away for yet another exotic cocktail without realizing how your bill is mounting up.

Bills were issued at the end of each leg of the World Cruise but I formed the habit of checking mine weekly so I could keep an eye on what I was spending. With five legs making up the 80 days my main fear was my expenditure would exceed my on board credit.

The other thing that was becoming noticeable was slight tension between some passengers who had previously been great friends. When several hundred people are thrown together in one environment for three months it is difficult not to get on each other's nerves.

I found I was avoiding people for a few days to try and give them some space as cruising is a very unnatural environment. After 28 days at sea I felt I had been away from home for months instead of weeks.

With no signal on my mobile phone, a hit-and-miss satellite system to send and receive emails and phone calls from the ship costing £5 a minute I did find I longed to hear a familiar voice and find out what was happening back in my home town of Newhaven in East Sussex.

DAY TWENTY SEVEN
Loneliness Becomes a Lover

Loneliness becomes a Lover –

Solitude a Darling Sin.

I cannot remember who wrote that but I do recall reading it somewhere and it has remained etched in my memory ever since.

Everyone thinks a cruise, especially a World Cruise is a wonderful, glamorous adventure, full of fun. But being on a ship 24 hours a day is not always a bed of roses and you can feel just as lonely in a crowd of people as you can when you live on your own in a tiny bed-sitting room.

Sharing a cabin with Janet helped me through the dark days and we had many a laugh. We both got very frustrated by the launderettes as certain passengers always hogged the driers so Janet resorted to drying her washing in our cabin.

But sometimes even Janet's brilliant sense of humour could not lift my spirits.

Janet with her washing in our cabin

Almost four weeks out of Southampton I experienced that feeling. Being a "singleton" like Bridget Jones I longed to be back home meeting my friends in my local pub, The Ark.

I longed to take my tiny Yorkshire Terries Tiffany for a walk along the West Quay and watch the Transmanche ferry set sail for Dieppe.

The daytime was fine. I played my usual game of shuffleboard, this time losing in the second round. This was quite opportune as the heavens opened just as I reached the bar by the swimming pool and all the ardent sunbathers made a bolt for shelter.

When it rains in the Pacific, it comes down hard. Although it is warm rain and it lasts a very short time you can get soaked in a matter of seconds.

The aftermath of the rain makes everything look dry very quickly and it is only when you lie on a sunbed without a towel beneath you you realise it is still wet. I made the mistake of forgetting my towel and lying in my bikini on my shorts and top only to have to walk back to my cabin with a big damp patch on my posterior hoping no-one would see me!

It was the evening that made me think of home. Being second sitting my dinner was at 8.30pm so there is a long time between coming off deck and going to the restaurant..

I had started to go to the sauna and steam room before getting showered but that still left the alternative of going to the bar or losing money on the slot machines.

I never felt uncomfortable sitting at any of the bars on my own as you can do this quite happily on a ship but it does increase your bar bill rapidly. As Nigel was bar manager he said he visited the Crow's Nest every night on his rounds and I used to sit on the same bar stool every night waiting for him to come. I looked forward to our nightly chats over a drink and never gave a thought to the reputation I was getting sitting at the bar waiting for "my officer" – a term used by my fellow passengers, not by me!

But what I did feel that particular night was the ship was made up of couples. Perhaps it was because the entertainment comprised of a round of Mr and Mrs and the audience was encouraged to compete on their own.

Amanda with Bar Manager Nigel Phillips

I recreated the scene in the Bridget Jones film when she sits on the sofa drinking wine listening to the record "All By Myself."

There is a misconception about cruising that you will automatically "meet someone" and have a steamy shipboard romance. Indeed there were passengers on the Oriana who had already paired off but I am very wary of shipboard romances.. I looked forward to meeting Nigel and I secretly hoped we might get closer before the end of the voyage. He seemed to enjoy my company as much as I enjoyed his even though I knew he had a girlfriend back home.

During our transit of the Panama Canal I met an 83-year-old American Karl Boehner. who asked me if I would like to share a hot tub with him that night, and I had also had a couple of other offers I had to refuse. I came on board determined to enjoy the trip and not get involved with anything that would complicate my travels. But sometimes you cannot help becoming attracted to someone, especially with the heady atmosphere of a cruise.

Shipboard life is very false. You live in a fantasy land where money never changes hands. Good looking officers appear in the evening in bum-hugging jackets that make your hormones turn circles and people who have just met suddenly walk around holding hands.

I dislike Singles Clubs, or anything with the word single in the title because I consider myself a person, whatever my marital status.

They do try to cater for lone travellers on P & O ships having special sessions for the singles and now they even have singles tables. But I have a personal hatred or being sidelined into a little box.I did go to one or two travelling alone get-togethers but they mostly consisted of elderly ladies who liked to play bridge every afternoon.

I found it easier to make friends by joining in the sports competitions I loved rather than sit around making small talk over a cup of coffee.

But for some reason, which is quite alien to me, I felt isolated and alone on the 27th evening of the cruise and I went to bed at 10.30pm hoping this frustrating interlude would soon pass and I could get back to the full enjoyment of my epic voyage.

Luckily my cabin-mate wanted to read for a while and I started looking at the in-house literature provided four weeks previously that I had not read before. I found out that on an average 14-day cruise the following items were consumed on board:

116,500 main meals are served, 15 tons of meat, 4 tons of fish, 7 tons of poultry and game, 3.5 tons of bacon/ham/gammon, 4.5 tons of butter/fat/cheese and 28 tons of fresh fruit and vegetables, 51,000 fresh eggs, 10,500 litres of milk and cream and 4,000 litres of ice cream, 70,000 bread rolls, 14,000 croissants and Danish pastries, 42,000 afternoon cakes and pastries, 4,200 white loaves and 1,400 brown loaves, 500 bottles of Champagne, 650 sparkling wine, 6,500 still wine, 2,500 spirits, 350 liquers, 420 port/sherry/vermouth, 200 gallons draught beer, 62,500 cans ale/stout/lager, 10,000 cans fruit juices, 28,500 cans minerals and cider and 3,000 bottles of mineral water.

Multiply those amounts by six to meet the needs of our 80 day voyage and you could imagine what the grocery bill must be like.

The average storage on the ship from Southampton is 170 tons so we collected extra provisions from various ports of call.

The Galley Brigade comprises 1 Execuitve Chef, 1 Premier Sous Chef, 2 Sous Chefs and 1 Junior Sous Chefs.

L Head Baker, 1 Executive Pastry Chef and 2 Pastry Chefs. L Chief Butcher, 4 Senior Chef De Parties, 9 Chef De Parties and 6 Junior Chef De Parties.

24 1st Commis, 7 2nd Commis, 13 3rd Commis and 20 Galley Assistants. There is also one Icae Carver who works exclusively on all the beautiful ice sculptures that appear at various gourmet events.

The galley caters for approximately 1,800 passengers and 805 crew.

DAY TWENTY EIGHT
CROSSING THE LINE

Four weeks after leaving a cold and wet Southampton Oriana Crossed the Line at 8.20am. The temperature was 84 degrees with the forecast promising it would get even hotter by the time the Official Ceremony took place in the afternoon.

In Oriana Today we received the following Proclamation:

"Permission is being sought for Oriana to cross the Equator during the daylight hours of Thursday February 3rd 2005.

"Word has been sent to Neptune Rex, Ruler of the Seven Seas, King of the Sector Currents, Lord of the Boundless Waves, Master of the High Tides, High Constable of the Coral Caverns and Uttermost Recesses of the Deep for us to be allowed to do so.

"A message has been received that he will visit Oriana together with the full Aquatic Court to give due consideration to this unusual request and carry out a most rigorous initiation ceremony into the ancient and moisturizing rites of the Call of the Conch and Nautilus. We understand that he will wish to hold court between the hours of 2.30 pm and 3.30 pm around the Riviera Pool. "

By 1.30 pm passengers were lining the decks above the pool ensuring they would get a good view. The Ceremony began with music to get us in the mood to celebrate by the guest band Powerhouse, and then King Neptune and his entourage arrived.

Challenging him to a fight to the death on the greasy pole was Staff Captain Charlie Carr and his team.

We were asked to cheer either for King Neptune or for the P & O team who were hoping to grab King Neptune's crown.

The sun shone down brilliantly as the members of each team aimed to knock their opponents off the pole with pillow cases containing water filled balloons.

Then came the final sorte between the King himself and the Staff Captain. Instead of one hit and instant surrender this was to be the best of three rounds. It was one all as the two enemies battled it out and the cheers must have been heard all over the South Pacific as the valiant Captain destroyed the King and took his crown.

I had crossed the equator before when I went to South Africa so I was already a subject of King Neptune's Court. In

1971 when I did it on the Union Castle ship the Vaal it was a different ceremony.

Then health and safety rules were not so stringent and passengers were used as victims. The ship's surgeons put raw liver in my bikini and raw eggs on my head then I was put in the ducking stool and tipped backwards into the pool.

King Neptune made a speech and we were enrolled as subjects of his kingdom. But the Crossing the Line Ceremony on Oriana was great fun for all the spectators

Everyone could be involved as they cheered for their team, not just the lucky passengers selected as victims.

Powerhouse continued to play as we swam beneath the greasy pole and the atmosphere round the ship was like New Year's Eve.

People continued the party mood into the evening when we were treated to Rave On by the Oriana Theatre Company. The production told the ups and downs of Buddy Holly's short life and we sang along with the cast as they gave us his greatest hits such as Rave On, Peggy Sue and Oh Boy.

Like the West End show Buddy it also included the Big Bopper and Richie Vallans singing La Bamba.

In just 24 hours I had suffered a whole gamut of emotions

that could only happen at sea. The highs and lows of going Round the World in 80 Days was making it an unforgettable trip.

DAY TWENTY NINE
La Balle Masque

There is a first time for everything on a ship and suddenly four weeks away from home, in the middle of the South Pacific, I acquired a Sugar Daddy.

Or I would have done if I had decided to take him up on his offer. The 83-year-old American I had met transitting the Panama Canal joined me at breakfast as he had been doing every day.

Karl would sit with Janet and I and make small talk but on that particular morning he was very quiet. When Janet left for her daily promenade round the deck he said could he ask me a question.

"Could I come and stay with you in England?" he said and I explained I was homeless as I had given up my rented flat to come on the cruise.

"That's no problem," he said. "I'll get the accommodation if I can come and stay with you."

Thinking it was a joke I expected him to laugh but he

looked as though he meant it. I decided it was time to make a hasty exit. I made a mental note to change my breakfast time in future.

KARL BOEHNER

As the cruise went on Karl and I became good friends and I discovered he was really quite harmless. But his offer had seemed very flattering at the time, even if I didn't take him up on it!

When I returned home he wrote to me regularly from America and I found I looked forward to his letters.

There was another first for me on the Oriana as the evening heralded a masked ball. I joined a group of ladies and two gentlemen to make something suitable to wear. But I cheated a bit as I had bought some Elton John star shaped sunglasses in Hawaii. They had bright red lenses and the frames depicted the American flag so I just added some red and black feathers and a couple of blue and white pipe cleaners..

The result was I looked like an alien from outer space but I was determined to join the parade of masks in the evening.

After lunch on a hot and oppressive afternoon I met up with singer/songwriter Gerard Kenny to talk about his life in the music business.

I had seen him on various British television shows like Les Dawson and chat shows so I was interested to learn more about his career.

His grandparents were Irish immigrants on both sides of the family and his father met his mother in New York.

His father Vincent was a song and dance man and performed in a soft shoe act The Three Joes in Vaudeville in the 1930s.

By the time Gerard was born in 1947 vaudeville was dead but he was surrounded by music from an early age as there was always music in the house.

"I walked up to the piano at the age of five and just started playing," he said. "I had heard my father playing so often it just came naturally to me."

He started composing when he was 14 years old when he was in a rock band and to be successful they had to write their own music.

At the age of 16 he was in the Phaetons Rock Band and they got their first recording contract with Warner Brothers.

"It was the time Billy Joel had his rock band," he said. "As you got older those without a calling dropped by the wayside. You don't choose this business, it chooses you."

In 1977 he had been working with lyricist Drey Shepperd for two years and Gerard wanted to play the gay clubs in New York as they were one of the few places where he could perform his own music.

"They had an open mike night on a Tuesday," he said "So I went down and paid my fee to sing two songs. The owner liked me and booked me for the opening two weeks with Leslie Gore (famous for the hit song It's My Party)."

One night an agent came in and asked Gerard if he would like to play in St Tropez. Gerard thought he was joking but after a follow-up meeting when he performed in a recording studio for 25 minutes he was contracted to go to La Papa Guyo, one of the top nightclubs in St Tropez.

Downstairs was a restaurant which Gerard turned into a piano bar and he became the success of the season.

"When I first started to play I had a grand piano and a synthesizer and I went in for a sound check one afternoon," he said.

"I saw lots of ramps in between the tables and a television camera and I asked what was going on. I was told there was to be a fashion show and I was to play for it."

Gerard had nothing prepared but when three girls came on in the evening in the skimpiest bikinis he played "That's Why The Lady is a Tramp" which brought the house down.

It was when he was playing the gay clubs in New York Barry Manilow came in to see the show and the two became friends. He composed "I made it through the rain," for Barry and often performs his songs in his act.

Going to his friend Dennis Waterman's birthday party in Chiswick in 1978 really changed his life.

"I met my manager, composed the theme for the television series Minder and signed a record deal with RCA," he said.

One of the conditions of the contract was he lived in England and on August 1 1978 he moved to the UK and stayed for nine years.

He went back to live in New York in 1987 but returned to England in 1997 when he became engaged to his second wife Jenny. They married in 1998 and now live in Ashdown Forest in Sussex, within walking distance of Pooh Bridge.

As well as his own recording contract Gerard has composed for artists such as Shirley Bassey, Perry Como and Johnny Mathis. He also wrote the music for Wayne Sleep's show Hot Shoe Shuffle.

He. has three boys from his first marriage who have all gone into the business.

"I think they are incredible," he said. "My third son Charlie is my engineer, my twins Jackson and Brandon have a group in New York called The Forms and they are doing very well.

He also inherited three boys from Jenny's first marriage and one of them Gordon has his own band in New York NSG.

"Don't ask me what it stands for, I have no idea," he said.

He loves cruising as he said it is the new vaudeville, the only place it still exists. He spends nine months of the year on the sea and he is happiest when he is tinkering at the piano in intimate surroundings.

"The Crow's Nest was an ideal venue," he said. "Just the right atmosphere.

Despite coming from the highest echelons of the music business Gerard is very much a people person.

He sunbathed on deck and was happy to talk to any of the passengers who approached him. Just as I finished the interview a man came up to arrange their golfing date the following morning when we were due to arrive in Pago Pago, American Samoa.

DAY THIRTY
Paradise Found – PAGO PAGO

Thirty days after leaving Southampton Oriana sailed into Paradise. From the moment I saw our approach to the American Samoan island at 6.30am I knew I had found my personal Shangri-La.

We were going into Pago Pago, the capital of Tutuila Island. Pronounced Pango Pango it ended up with its present name because the missionaries who first came there had no N in their printing kit.

Woods extend down to the sea, with hotels and houses nestling amongst the trees. The Samoan culture is Polynesia's oldest and the first people on the Samoan Islands came by sea some 3,000 years ago.

Over the centuries distinct cutltural traits emerged and seafaring explorers and settlers journeyed to other Polynesian island groups hundred of miles away.

As we stepped off the ship we were greeted by a display of

traditional song and dance which is an integral part of Samoa and I met Miss American Samoa, one of the most beautiful women I have ever seen.

Miss American Samoa and two of the dancers.

Stalls with brightly coloured sarongs and shirts lined the quay and I bought a coconut which a Polynesian girl took from an icebox and deftly chopped the top off with a knife so I could drink the milk.

I decided to go first to the beach which was five minutes walk from the ship. It was there I found my own personal paradise. After the disappointment of Hawaii here was what I had been looking for.

A palm-fringed beach of golden sand with the crystal clear waters of the South Pacific which was very warm but also refreshing when you swam further out to sea.

All it needed was Rosanna Brazzi to come galloping up the beach on his white horse and I could have "Washed That Man Right Out of my Hair!"

I spent nearly two hours on the beach before walking slowly back to the ship. Near the beach was the Rainmaker Hotel, dubbed the worst hotel in the South Pacific.

It is now owned by the Government who is desperately trying to sell it. The hotel has been closed for a year having gone into liquidation and I was able to go inside and have a look round.

It was very sad to see what once must have been a luxury hotel in such a sad state of repair. There were torn carpets and abandoned furniture everywhere. In the right hands it could once again be a jewel in Pago Pago's crown.

I saw Eva Bartok in Somerset Maugham's play Rain many years ago. But I did not know until February 5 2005 that Sadie Thompson was a real person. I thought she was a character created by Maugham for his splendid play.

She lived in Pago Pago where she seduced the young curate and caused his downfall and I visited the house where she used to live. Above the bar was a poster of the film which starred Joan Crawford. Rita Heyworth also played the notorious lady of ill repute in an old black and white movie.

I discovered Jurassic Park was filmed on the island and looking at the rainforests stretching almost to the sea I could see why.

The volcanic island of Tutuila is the largest of the seven islands that comprise American Samoa. We docked in Pago Pago Harbour which is a collapsed volcanic caldera and one of the largest natural harbours in the South Pacific.

From the ship we had a clear view of Fatu-ma-futi, known as The Flower Pot Island that stands at the mouth of the harbour.

The local legend is that a man and a pregnant woman were trying to reach Tutuila but failed to do so. She nearly got there safely but the man was further out when he drowned.

She was carrying a baby boy and three islands were named the male island, female island and one after the baby. The male Flower Pot Island is the largest and one of the island's landmarks.

Just before we sailed we were treated to another performance by the dancers culminating in a spectacular dance by Miss American Samoa in a huge wig. Passengers lined up to press dollar bills into her hand before we had to say farewell to these lovely people and board the ship to set sail for Tonga.

It was with a heavy heart I watched my paradise disappear from view and I hoped one day I might return.

DAY THIRTY-ONE
The Day That Never Was

This was the day of rest and recovery following the scorching heat in Pago Pago. Sun loungers remained empty as people sought the shady areas of the ship. Passengers were still discussing their day in paradise and looking forward to Tonga the following day.

Another topic of conversation all over the ship was the day that never was. The thirty-first day out of Southampton was Sunday February 6.

We would go to bed as normal, doing nothing to our watches, and wake up on Tuesday February 8th. So for us Monday February 7th 2005 never existed.

In the early hours of the morning of 9th February Oriana would cross the International Date Line. In order to align date and time with that on the other side of the Date Line it was necessary for us to lose a day.

Three members of the ship's company and six passengers were due to celebrate their birthdays on February 7th so their photographs were featured in Oriana Today and a special get-together was held for them..

But before we lost a day the Oriana Theatre Company were due to present a Mardi Gras show on deck by the swimming pool.

The rig of the night was sarongs and flowers in our hair so the entertainment staff laid on a session to show the different ways to tie a sarong and one how to make a hibiscus for your hair.

I made two beautiful flowers but the problem was the stems were so thick and my hair so short it was impossible to fix them in. In the end in frustration I threw them in the bin and went to the shop to buy a flower.

The show was full of fun and expertly performed as usual and then a disco started so we could all dance on deck.

I saw two elderly ladies jigging about together having a wonderful time. One of them clutched two balloons and wouldn't let them go, even when dancing.

One of the highlights was a long conga line which wound its way round the pool. No-one within grabbing distance of the dancers was safe, even the officers who gamely joined in.

We partied into the night knowing when we woke up we would all be two days older instead of one.

DAY THIRTY-TWO
TONGA – The Friendly Isles.

We were supposed to be anchored out at sea in Nuku'Alofa, on the island of Tongatapu, but at the last minute the Captain was told we could go alongside.

The approach was not nearly as pretty as Pago Pago and the port was very industrial, half-an-hour's walk from the town.

As we arrived at the quayside the Tonga Police Band played us in with a delightful variety of music including an Elvis Presley melody, Waltzing Matilda and several old English favourite tunes.

The ship was cleared very quickly and because of the rising temperatures we decided the best plan was to go ashore as soon as possible.

As a young child I clearly remember sitting on the balcony of my father's club, The United Services in Pall Mall, and watching the Coronation procession of Queen Elizabeth II. The one thing I remember most was the beaming face of Queen Salote of Tonga who was wearing a tall feather which gradually collapsed in the pouring rain.

I wanted to see the Royal Palace where her son Taufa'ahau Tupou IV, now lives. It was a long walk from the ship along the palm-fringed shoreline.

I passed a few very unusual cemeteries on the way where the Tongans bury their dead above ground in mounds covered by gravel.

The grave in Tonga

Most of the graves had painted screens behind them and there was one very elaborate grave covered with very large wreaths of colourful flowers.

Asking a Tongan lady whose grave it was I learnt that it

was the wife of a high-up Government official who died in December 2004. She had a big family who regularly put flowers on her grave.

I passed the white Treasury building before turning the corner to reach the Royal Palace. No flag was flying so I presumed the King was not in residence.

The handsome white palace was built in 1867 and has Norfolk pines and lawns spreading down to the road by the waterfront. The verandah to the second storey was added in 1882 when the Royal Chapel was built.

Sadly the palace is not open to the public and the closest I could get was in the field by the locked gates and high wire fence.

I walked on into the town and the difference in economy was very noticeable. Pago Pago in American Samoa receives a large subsidy from the American Government, Tonga is independent and is struggling to survive.

The town is run-down, although there were one or two nice shops. I bought a pair of sandals which pleased my cabin-mate as my old sandals had been through an English summer before supporting my feet through the heat of the cruise.

Tonga is known as the Friendly Isles and I could see why. The people were lovely and very anxious to talk to us.

I took a picture of a woman who looked just like Bloody

Amanda Wilkins

Mary in South Pacific. She gave me a beaming smile and instead of asking for money she took a shell necklace from round her neck and gave it to me. "Here is a present from our island," she said.

The Bloody Mary lookalike Tonga

Colourful stalls were set up along the dockside and the main items were basketwork and carved wooden figures and marks.

Much to Janet's dismay I arrived back in the cabin with a three-foot high carved wooden mask. Made out of mahogany it is typical Tongan work and beautifully carved by the father of the stallholder. How I would get it off the ship in Southampton was something I would have to face at the end of the cruise.

Tapa-making and mat weaving are the major occupations of the female population and mats and tapa cloths were in abundance on the quay.

Tapa is made from the inner bark of the mulberry tree, which is beaten out with a mallet. Mats are the most treasured possessions in Tongan households and are given on special occasions. The Tongans mostly wear them round their waists.

In the afternoon, despite the heat, I decided to walk back into town along Vuna Road as I wanted to once again meet these lovely, friendly people.

I was told to go and see the Tonga Visitors Bureau as it is a fine example of the skill of local craftsmen.

Known as fale, it was built in 1978 in traditional style with four kinds of wood. The walls and inside of the roof are covered with two layers of the thicker tofua leaf and the finer weave of pandanus.

I was fascinated to see typical Tongan scenery depicted on each pattern and I was told thirty eight palm trees were used for the roof covering.

Inside the bureau is decorated with nearly 100 square yards of embroidered tapa cloth and there are two thirteen foot carved totem poles standing at the entrance, presented by the people of New Zealand.

Of all the ports we had been to so far the sailing from Tonga was the most emotional. The band played us out whilst the quay was lined with people waving and calling "We love you" which brought the response from the passengers "We love you too."

Somehow the evening's entertainment on the ship – another open air Hoedown – seemed pale in comparison and I shed a tear as I went to bed knowing I had left the South Pacific behind.

DAY THIRTY-THREE
Loser Takes All

Thirty-three days out of Southampton
I excelled myself in my failures on board Oriana.

I began playing Shuffleboard and was outstandingly beaten in the first round having scored nothing at all.

I moved on to Short Tennis, which ten years ago I taught on board the P & O liner Canberra. I had not touched a racket for two years and it took me a bit of time to get back into the game. But my partner and I managed to draw level at two games all and we lost in a sudden death deuce in the decider.

I then moved on to the specialist quiz on "Who Said That" and got ten out of twenty. But it was in the afternoon I had my most spectacular loss of all time.

I volunteered to take part in Adult Fun in the Sun, commonly known as aquatic sports in the old cruising days. With fond memories of diving for spoons, which I am fairly good at, I was the first to put my name down.

I was allocated to entertainment officer Malcolm Lawrence's team, the only woman in a line up of five, four of whom were burly Australians.

We were up against the team headed by entertainment officer Gary Morris and they also had one woman and four men.

I cannot do the crawl and I had no idea the first event would be a relay race. My breast stroke against my opponent's crawl put us behind from the start.

Then I had to face her on the greasy pole. We had to bash each other anywhere except the head with a pillow case containing a water-filled balloon. It was not an easy task and she was like a rock. I managed to hold my ground until we each had to put one foot on the pole. One hit and she tipped me into the water.

Other events included swimming in a boiler suit and after two widths of the pool I was stripped by my team mates so the next one could be dressed in the suit.

I took some heart at my dreadful performance when Gary tipped Malcolm into the water as well with great ease when they faced each other on the greasy pole.

It was all good fun but in the evening I proudly showed off

my battle scars, a burn-mark on my arm from the pole when I fell off and a painful elbow.

I will volunteer for anything but I decided this was not my forte and not something I would put my name down for in the next leg of the trip.

The actors gave their first performance of Don't Dress For Dinner for first sitting passengers and those that saw it thoroughly enjoyed it..As my dinner was second sitting my performance would be the following day..

Instead I went to Gerard Kenny's last show which this time was in a packed Pacific Lounge.

Each of his performances was completely different. On stage he gave a polished cabaret, in the Crow's Nest he played music for a piano bar and on this night it was loud, brash and funny.

I was very sorry that he was leaving the ship at Sydney but was thankful P & O's other ship Aurora, due to do a mammoth voyage, had broken down as he was scheduled to do the cabaret on her.

News of her disaster had filtered through to us from the moment we left Southampton. She had been due to sail two days after us for a Grand Voyage round South America lasting

103 nights.

She broke down in Lisbon en route to Southampton and the sailing was postponed for two days. She had to undergo sea trials and the passengers, who paid from £10,000 – £60,000 for the trip, were taken twice round the Isle of Wight.

They eventually set off from Southampton on their Grand Voyage ten days late only to turn back because they could not get up enough speed for the round trip.

Gerard told me the passengers had free drinks 24-hours a day, top class entertainers like Elaine Page and Paul Daniels and they were taken by coach to London to see the shows.

They were also heavily compensated for the loss of their trip but I tried to imagine my disappointment had this happened to me.

When you plan a trip like mine, down to the minutest detail, it would have been heartbreaking to have to abandon it at the eleventh hour.

My furniture had been farmed out, as had my spare clothes, books, videos and even my dog.

My friends who were looking after Tiffany had been sending me letters from her to various ports telling me she was getting fat as she had developed a liking for Guinness. The second letter I received told me she had moved on to gin and asked where was her card!

The mad world I was living in had obviously affected my friends back home. Luckily the black dog that had sat on my chest for two days after being so long at sea had got off and my spirits were rising as I anticipated my first ever sight of Australia in four days' time.

I was further away from home than I had ever been in my life and had lost count of what time or even what day it was back home. We had travelled half-way round the world and seen eight ports.

But sixteen more were to come including Vietnam, Hong Kong and Singapore. We had still not been told if we were going to Phuket following the tragic tsunami that had virtually wiped out the resort. All we had been told was they were desperate to get the tourists back but it would depend if there was any disease there following the giant tidal wave.

Thailand was one of the highlights of the itinerary and I was devastated when I saw the destruction on Boxing Day. But the Captain had the health and safety of Oriana passengers to consider and we were all happy to bide by his final decision..

DAY THIRTY-FOUR
Don't Dress For Dinner

I have loved theatre ever since I was taken to see my first pantomime, Dick Whittington, when I was four years old.

But I never expected to walk into a theatre on a ship and see a properly furnished stage set with a cast worthy of any West End production.

It was the first time I had seen a play at sea as I have always watched shows before with beautiful costumes and minimal sets.

But on February 10th I sat in the front row of Oriana's Theatre Royal and watched for free a farce that would have cost me £40 in London.

Don't Dress For Dinner had a superb cast, Frazer Hines, Robert Duncan and the two girls from Allo Allo, Vicki Michelle and Sue Hodge. Making up the cast were two members of

Oriana's resident theatre company Colette Bibby and Jacob Chapman.

The production was very slick and the timing excellent. Laughter resounded all round the theatre and it was an unusual and welcome addition to our shipboard entertainment.

The four actors came on board in Hawaii to do two plays, the second being Bedside Manners, which would be performed on the next leg of the World Cruise.

On Day thirty-four we had mixed weather as we approached New Zealand. It was hot in the morning but very windy then the rain came in the afternoon.

Another new innovation was slotted into the entertainment programme when deputy cruise director Carla led a lesson in social party dances.

I already knew how to do the Gay Gordons, St Bernard's Waltz and Barn Dance but the Marengi and Party Samba were new to me.

My knowledge of the Marengi was taken from the film Dirty Dancing when Patrick Swayze was trying to teach it to "Baby" in a very short time.

Carla's version was not as risqué as the one danced by Patrick Swayze but as I danced it with the female entertainment officer Adele I didn't really mind the sexy dancing being left out!

My intention had been to go to the special session in the evening to put into practice what I had learnt, but sense prevailed and I decided to go to bed at 10.15pm straight after dinner in preparation for the day ahead.

It would be my first visit to New Zealand and my debut crewing an America's Cup Yacht. I was inspired for my excursion by the Oriana's potted version of the Daily Mail received on February 10.

I read that Great Britain's youngest and newest Dame, Ellen MacArthur, had sailed into Falmouth to a tumultuous welcome after becoming the fastest solo non-stop round-the-world sailor in history.

Ellen had completed her voyage in 71 days, 14 hours, 18 minutes and 33 seconds. This was 32 hours and 33 minutes faster than Frenchman Francis Joyon who had previously held the record.

It seemed incredible that this slip-of-a-girl could do this in her 75ft trimaran B & Q, knowing the seas we had been through in our gigantic liner.

DAY THIRTY-FIVE
"We are Sailing....."

For the first time, even though I went to bed early, I missed our approach to Auckland. By the time I got up on deck at 7am we were edging into the quay. My fellow passengers who had been up since 5am told me how beautiful it had been and I was cross with myself that I had failed to make it..

At 9.15am I left the ship for what was to turn out to be the most exciting experience of my life.

We walked the short distance to the America's Cup yacht berth and for the first time I saw the boat in which I would be sailing.

NZL40 is 75ft long, the same as Ellen MacArthur's, but a third of the width of her trimaran.

Being a racing yacht there was nothing on board except the ropes, turning handles for the sails and other equipment.

We were given a brief safety talk by the young men who were taking us out for the morning and issued with inflatable life jackets. Then we were invited to step aboard.

NZL 40

This was very much a hands-on excursion where we were expected to work and as soon as we had motored out into the harbour the skipper called for "grinders".

With two of us to each handle we had to wind backwards and

forwards as instructed to raise the large sail. It was hard work even for two of us and I wondered how Ellen had managed to do it single-handed on her boat as she sailed round the world.

It was perfect sailing weather and we soon picked up speed reaching 10 knots at one point. I had often seen these racing yachts on television tilted to an extreme angle but I had never experienced it.

For a lot of the trip we were at an angle of 30 degrees and when I went to take a photograph I had to grab the hand of one of the crew to haul me back up across the boat.

NZL40 had been built for the French team entry in the 1995 America's Cup and is now used to take people out in Auckland so they can get a taste of what it is like to sail in a racing yacht.

New Zealand has won the cup three times, losing it in the last competition to Italy. They are determined to win it back in 2007 and we saw the boat which will compete in the race training in the harbour.

We had a wonderful view of the city and also two impressive volcanic cones, Mount Eden (Maori name Mongaawhau) which is 600 feet about sea level and One Tree Hill (Maori name Maungaklekie).

This was the largest and most populous of the Maori settlements and at the top is the grave of the prominent pioneer

Sir John Logan Campbell, known as "the Father of Auckland".

We sailed down the harbour before turning round past the ship and going under the road bridge. As we approached it we looked as if the sail was going to hit the central span but we glided under with just three metres to spare.

Returning to the quay I was allowed to take the wheel and as we faced the bridge for the second time I asked a member of the crew if he wanted to take over.

"No, you can take it through," he said and I had total control of the boat. As we sailed between the central stantions I felt it was the proudest moment of my life.

The Author at the wheel of NZL 40

All too soon the trip was over but they told me I could return and crew for them anytime. I did consider jumping ship but I had to achieve my dream and go round the world in 80 days!

The afternoon seemed pale in comparison as I explored the city. With wide streets dominated by skyscrapers it must be one of the most modern cities in the world.

I visited the famous All Blacks' shop but couldn't afford a rugby shirt so I settled for a stuffed kiwi wearing one instead.

Returning to the ship in the early evening we were treated to a Maori Cultural Show given by local singers and dancers.

Dressed in traditional costume the menacing warriors were a strong contrast to the beautiful girls in their beaded skirts.

When they asked for volunteers I was invited up to do a dance with them spinning a leather ball on the end of a corded string. I was told I was very good at spinning and catching it in the other hand but found spinning it in a figure of eight much more difficult.

The weather deteriorated in the afternoon and it rained as we sailed away but the misty drizzle that shrouded the distant shore seemed to make it even more magical and I could see why Auckland is known as the "City of Sails".

My sail has left a mark on me that I will not forget. It was a once-in-a-lifetime experience that few are lucky enough to do.

DAY THIRTY SIX
The Good Old Bad Old Days

We had a shock on day thirty-six when we were called to an extra tap class and told we were performing in front of an audience at the Chiefly Yourselves Talent Show the following night.

We spent an hour going over and over the routine we had learnt to the CD Something Stupid and at the end we agreed we were ready to give it a go.

My newly acquired tap shoes from a ballet shop in Auckland gave me confidence as I could hear the steel plates reverberating on the dance floor.

It was not easy as the ship was moving quite a lot due to the wind but at least none of us fell over.

I went to the Crow's Nest after rehearsal and listened to a first-class tribute to ragtime king Scott Joplin from Allen Brooks at the piano.

The talk round the ship was about the news we had received

that HRH the Prince of Wales was to marry Camilla Parker Bowles on April 8 at Windsor Castle.

All the Australians wanted to know the Brits opinion and everyone had their own views.

Queues formed at the reception desk as people lined up to get their Australian dollars for the next three ports of call, Sydney, Brisbane and the Whitsunday Islands. I only had twenty New Zealand dollars left which brought me fifteen Australian dollars.

The evening's entertainment was a show I had not seen from the talented Oriana Theatre Company, The Good Old Bad Old Days.

This was a joyous celebration of being British and the performers gave a light-hearted stroll through time recalling people, places, famous inventions, engineering feats and sporting heroes.

There were also tributes to politicians and members of the Royal Family including the late Princess Diana, which brought a round of applause.

We were all handed Union Jacks as we went into the Theatre Royal and the climax was the whole audience on their feet singing Land of Hope and Glory with great gusto. Everyone in the auditorium joined in, the Brits, Australians, Americans and Canadians.

In Harlequins the Farewell Ball was being held to mark the end of the second leg of the cruise, which seemed to have gone much faster than the first.

It seemed strange to say goodbye to a large number of Australian friends who had joined the ship at Southampton and I was very sad to see some of them go. This included a rotund little man called Harry Cooper who had taught me to jive and who had been a great dancing partner .His wife Irene had recently had an operation and was not allowed to dance so she lent Harry to me on several occasions!

It was with a heavy heart I realized a major part of my journey was now over but with it came the realization that we were not yet half way through the trip.

DAY THIRTY-SEVEN
Tapping the Night Away

Everyone assumes when you go on a cruise you have fun twenty-four hours a day for the duration of the cruise. But there are days when extreme boredom sets in and you could scream at having to do the same things again and again.

My life on board had become a long round of shuffleboard, daily tote, bingo – sometimes – eating and drinking and days thirty-seven and thirty-eight were 48 hours of wishing something would happen to break the routine.

The tap dancing display was a welcome interlude and following a most enjoyable lunch with Nigel I decided to try something different – deck quoits.

I had played it years ago when I cruised with my parents but had not attempted it on this cruise.

When the names were drawn out of the hat I was partnered with a quoits regular Ivor and amazingly we won round after round until we reached the final.

We were playing to twenty-one points and it was a real needle match with both pairs standing at twenty when I had the last quoit to throw. I couldn't believe it when I scored two making us the winners and giving me my first prize after six weeks of trying.

But little did I know the repercussions of my win. I became the most hated woman on the ship. I had encroached on the territory inhabited by the quoits regulars and stolen the best player as my partner.

Janet was told at dinner I had only won my P & O umbrella because I played with Ivor and I knew I would never dare visit the deck quoits court again.

We had a rehearsal for the Talent Show with the other entrants and we decided as a team of four to wear sparkly tops and black trousers so we would look co-ordinated.

We hoped by drawing attention to our tops the audience would not look at our inexperienced feet. We also arranged to come out of dinner early so we could sneak in a private rehearsal in Decibels, the youngsters nightclub, at 10pm before the show started.

We had started off as six plus our instructor, entertainment officer Elaine, but one hurt her knee and another went down with flu so we ended up as four.

Being thrown together in this situation had bonded us all together and Dawn, Sandi, Margaret and myself had great fun as we performed warm-up exercises on the bar outside the room, much to the amusement of our fellow passengers going in to see the show.

We were third on after a duet sung by two passengers who had met on the Aurora and Paddy Masefield, an ME sufferer in a wheelchair who told some moving stories.

David and Carla, the entertainment officers in charge of the show gave us a brief introduction before Elaine and the Oriana Tappers took to the stage.

We went through our routine twice before being called back to give a second bow. I was astonished to find actor Frazer Hines had come to watch me for once, instead of me watching him and he told me he enjoyed it.

The tappers were all doing the entire World Cruise so we said just wait till you see us at the end of the last leg.

The show was quite short so we were able to see the end of the Farewell Variety Show given by the professionals in the Theatre Royal and I was very sad to think I was seeing Gerard Kenny for the last time.

Then we rushed round the ship to find Australian friends

and swap addresses before they left for good early the following day.

Cases were placed outside cabins as six hundred people prepared to leave the ship at Sydney. This latest leg of the cruise had seemed to go remarkably quickly and was more noticeable than the end of the previous leg.

DAY THIRTY-EIGHT
SYDNEY

This was the day I had been waiting for –

my first sight of Australia.

I got up at 5.30am to see us arrive in what was reputed to be one of the loveliest cities in the world and I was not disappointed.

As I had my first sight of the Sydney Harbour Bridge and the famous opera house tears of emotion trickled down my face. At last I had reached what I knew would become my spiritual home. Blessed with the world's prettiest natural harbour I noticed extensive bushland and many harbour islands as we sailed through the heads.

Fellow Australian passengers pointed out places like Manley on the starboard side and the pendulous bridge that links two sides of the city.

The opera house was just as impressive as I thought it would be with its fantastic white sails towering above the sea.

We docked at Circular Quay, right in the centre of the town and from my cabin window I had a clear view of the opera house.

Sydney Opera House

The colourful U-shaped quay, wedged between the opera house and The Rocks, is the hub of Sydney's water traffic and ferry services.

It is lined with quality restaurants and is bustling with commuters and buskers. The first thing that struck me when I went ashore was how clean and vibrant the city was and I knew immediately I would love to live there.

I first went to visit Sydney Harbour Bridge, affectionately

known by the locals as The Coathanger. Completed in 1932 for decades it provided the only permanent link between the two sides of the harbour until the opening of the harbour tunnel.

Janet on deck with Sydney Harbour Bridge in the background

There is a pedestrian walkway or for the more energetic you could book to do a bridge climb. I enquired about this but as I suffer from claustrophobia they would not allow me to do it.

To get on to the bridge itself you have to go through a long narrow tunnel in groups of twelve and the rules are very strict.

Everyone has to fill in a questionnaire, be breathalised and have a metal detector run over them before they are issued with a silver suit and a harness to do the three-hour climb.

After they rejected my application I walked round Circular Quay to the opera house and found at close quarters it is one of the most striking buildings I have ever seen.

The complex boasts nearly 1,000 rooms and it is one of the busiest arts centres in the world.

The roof which forms the sails is all tiled which is not obvious until you are close up to it and sitting on the steps leading up to the top I realized I felt happier than I had been for a very long time.

The highlight of my visit to Sydney was my shore excursion to see Opera Australia perform Carmen.

It is wonderful to find an opera house where the audience still dresses up for the performance. Wearing my smartest black cocktail dress I got into the limousine at the terminal which was to take us to the opera.

We were all allocated tickets and a programme and I was in the dress circle. Climbing over 200 steps to reach the top I was overwhelmed by the views.. We could go out on to the terrace one side or look through the glass windows towards the bridge on the other.

This was a large scale production with a large chorus as well as a childrens' chorus. Conducted by Alexander Polianichko from Russia, Carmen was brilliantly sung by an American Andrea Baker.

The two male leads, Don Jose and the toreador Escamillo were sung beautifully by Julian Gavin from Australia and New Zealander Teddy Tahu Rhodes.

I had seen Carmen before but never on this scale and it was one of the most brilliant productions I had ever seen. In the final death scene when she is shot by Don Jose she slid down the wall of the bull ring leaving a trail of blood behind her.

The cheers that resounded round the opera house sent a shiver down by spine and as I walked round Circular Quay back to the ship I felt happier and more exhilerated than I had done for several months.

A deck party was in full swing when I got back in

Amanda Wilkins

preparation for our midnight sailing. Coming into Sydney had been wonderful but leaving at night and seeing the lights fade into the distance was something special.

Here was a place I wanted to live more than anywhere else in the world and I knew it was the place I would eventually return to. I didn't know how as the giant liner glided out of the harbour but I had to find a way.

DAY THIRTY NINE
Half-way point.

This was almost the half-way stage of my Round The World voyage.

We had been on M.V. Oriana for thirty nine days and we had forty one days to go.

I had got over my blues about being on board for so long and looked forward to seeing Asia and India after leaving Australia.

The thirty-ninth day on board was also a red letter day for me because at the seventh attempt I actually won a shuffleboard final with the help of my partner Ronnie.

I had tried for so long to win a final I couldn't believe it when I was handed another P & O umbrella!

The approach to Brisbane was very windy but it was a warm wind and we had a clear view of the Australian coastline as we sailed along.

It was a strange day on board with very little activity in

the evening. There was a performance in the Theatre Royal by comedian, vocalist and instrumentalist Steve Stevens and a karaoke evening in the Lords Tavern.

I allowed myself to be led astray by an Australian couple in the casino and lost £30 on the roulette table very quickly.

It was a silly thing to do with so many more days to go but I did have fun doing it. I was sorry my new-found friendship was so short-lived as they were due to get off the ship the following morning in Brisbane.

The Australian passengers certainly brightened up the cruise. Although they were quite noisy and brash I loved them and soon warmed to everyone I met.

Being an outgoing person I knew I would have a great affinity with Australia and would be sorry when we finally sailed from Queensland after the Whitsunday Islands on February 18th.

I joined Frazer Hines for a drink after my dismal gambling failure but we both declined an invitation to sing on the karaoke.

Being tone deaf I would have quickly cleared the room had I had a go. Most people, myself included, decided not to stay up too late as we were due to sail into Brisbane early the following morning.

I had waited so long to come to Australia, now our visit was going far too quickly.

DAY FORTY
BRISBANE

On the half-way point of my round the world trip we sailed into Brisbane.

Positioned in Queensland in the middle of Australia's east coast it is already the third largest city in the country and well on the way to becoming Australia's second largest capital city within the next ten years.

We had been told we would be berthed a long way from the town and shuttle buses would take us into the city.

I had expected the approach to be very commercial so I was surprised to see fields and trees interspersed with the refineries and other business buildings.

The port itself was nothing but a yard where the coaches waited to take us into town and on the shore excursions. From the stern of the ship I could see the high speed CityCat which operates a ferry service from Brett's Wharf, Hamilton to the

University of Queensland at St Lucia.

It stopped en route at major attractions including North Quay in the City and I thought it would be fun to travel into town on that.

I aimed to catch the 10am ferry but when I enquired on shore I found Brett's Wharf was too far to walk so I joined four other passengers to take a taxi there.

We arrived to find the gates were shut because the CityCat was full so we decided to continue into the city centre by taxi which cost us five Australian dollars each.

Brisbane's downtown precinct is compact and easily accessible on foot. The central shopping hub is Queen Street Mall which boasts over 650 stores in a stretch of less than one kilometre..

I found masses of shoe shops, many of them selling very expensive footwear, even when they had a sale.

In contrast there were discounted souvenir shops where I was able to buy presents for friends at home and Quilpie Opals where I purchased a silver white opal ring.

Australia is famous for its opals and the one I bought was mined in Andamooka in South Australia. It has a light milky base with a sparkling array of pastel colours on the face of the stone.

I had always heard the myth that opals were unlucky unless you were born in October but I decided to risk it even though I was born in December.

When I had finished my shopping I went to look at the Conrad Treasury Casino which was once home to the state's coiffers..

The historic Treasury Building now rings with the sound of the roulette wheel and more than 1200 gaming machines.

It occupies three levels of this ornate Italian Renaissance styled building and has one hundred gaming tables and several restaurants and bars.

The Meyer Centre is a huge indoor shopping centre off the Queen Street Mall with six floors of shops and restaurants.

It was certainly worth a visit as it is very well designed with more than two hundred specialist shops, a diverse food court and a new cinema complex that opened in November 2001.

What struck me most in all the shopping malls was the friendly and helpful staff who would go out of their way to assist you, unlike some of the staff in the shops back home.

I walked down from Queen Street to King George Square to have a look at City Hall. There was a free tour to the top of the clock tower which gave a new perspective of the city.

Waterways are the lifeblood of Brisbane which is built around the winding river and it is the only city in Australia with a beach right in the Downtown area at South Bank.

Driving back to the ship we passed the Parliament House and the City Botanic Gardens. Established in 1824 it was originally built as a fruit and vegetable garden to supply the fledgling Moreton Bay penal settlement.

Now it features twenty hectares of flowers and trees including huge Moreton Bay figs and a mango boardwalk.

What I found very unusual was the amount of greenery in the City Centre. Concrete buildings stood side by side with lawns and trees which prevents Brisbane from becoming a concrete jungle.

I wept tears of sadness to be leaving Australia when we sailed from Brisbane at 6pm. We still had the Whitsunday Islands to come but I felt very sad at leaving behind the two Australian cities I had enjoyed so much.

It was spectacular watching Oriana sail under the Goodwill Bridge as there seemed a very small gap between the top of the funnel and the bottom of the bridge.

An engineering marvel the bridge straddles the Brisbane River to join the City Botanic Gardens and Queensland

University of Technology to Southbank near the Maritime Museum.

It is credited as being the longest pedestrian and cycle bridge in the world at 450 metres and was named after the successful sporting spectacle hosted by Brisbane in 2001, the Goodwill Games.

I don't know if it is the glorious weather that makes everyone smile in Australia or if it is because they are genuinely happy people. All I know is that in the two days I had spent in Sydney and Brisbane I found myself feeling happier and more content than I had felt for a very long time.

I used to be very proud to be British and could not imagine living anywhere else but seeing so much of the world made me realize how much we have sunk into a depression in England and how much our green and pleasant land has declined over the years.

DAY FORTY ONE
Welcome Aboard

Another day at sea made a welcome interlude between the two Australian cities and the Whitsunday Islands.

It was extremely hot and I was glad I did not survive too many rounds of shuffleboard. The individual quiz was on horse racing but it was not my forte and I only managed to scrape together a meagre seven points out of twenty.

In the afternoon the shop on board staged a fashion show round the pool and we were able to watch the entertainment officers modeling swimwear and reversible dresses that could be worn afternoon and evening.

Even after forty days on board this was a new addition to the entertainment programme and preceded the Fun in the Sun competition.

This time I did not volunteer to take part and I was very pleased to see there was another female passenger who was as bad as I was in the pool and on the greasy pole.

But watching it I realized the score does not matter, it is a good spectator event providing lots of fun and I thought I might give it another go on the next leg.

As we had been at sea for six weeks my hair had become thicker and out of control..I try to avoid hair salons on board ship if possible as they are more expensive than at home but needs must and I put myself in the hands of a South African stylist Lindsey.

It was the most fun I have ever had at a hairdressers and we never stopped laughing. She convinced me I needed a couple of products to maintain the first-class style she had conceived for my hair and I went away poorer but happier.

Having just started another leg of the cruise the Captain was holding his Welcome Aboard parties and this was my third.

The parties follow the same format every time and the ship's officers must hate them. There are four parties each time, two for the first sittings in the two restaurants and two for the second sitting.

Those dining in the Oriental Restaurant go to the Pacific Lounge and those in the Peninsular Restaurant where I was dining go to the Crow's Nest which I think is the nicer venue because of the outstanding views.

I decided after dinner to go and see Follies again by the Oriana Theatre Company and it was even better second time around.

Even though we had another six weeks on board the ship I still began to feel that now we were leaving Australia we were on our way home.

Then I remembered how long we had been at sea and realized we had the equivalent of the same time again and some great ports of call to visit.

DAY FORTY TWO
Whitsunday Islands.

You have bad days and you have good days -
and you have very bad days you wish to forget.

February 18 2005 was one of those disastrous days that I would like to erase from my memory forever, but it will be difficult.

Oriana anchored in CID Harbour, off Hamilton Island early in the morning. It is one of 74 tropical islands in the Whitsunday group and the largest of the 12 inhabited islands.

It lies in the Coral Sea between the Queensland Coast and the Great Barrier Reef and our approach was very pretty.

More than eighty per cent of the island is natural tropical bushland, and the greenery of the other islands dotted round our anchorage was lush and plentiful.

The excursion to the Great Barrier Reef was expensive and took a long time because the reef was approximately 45 miles from our anchorage.

Instead I opted to go by catamaran and glass bottom boat to Bali Hai because the name reminded me of South Pacific.

It is a World Heritage Listed Marine Reserve and the island is uninhabited. Because of logistical problems at the last minute the tour excursions office changed both the itinerary and the timings of my tour.

The new timings would have meant taking an entire chunk out of the day and with a 6pm sailing I would have had no chance to explore Hamilton Island.

There was supposed to be a lovely beach within five minutes walk from the landing stage or you could hire a golf buggy to explore the area.

Because of the change of timings I obtained a refund for my tour and arranged to go ashore with Carol and Ted who were on my table.

The 25-minute trip from the ship to the island was by local tender but the Australian authorities had underestimated the number of people wishing to go ashore from Oriana.

With a full ship carrying approximately 1800 passengers even taking away those booked on official excursions it still left about 1,000 wanting to go ashore by tender..

All crew leave was stopped to allow the passengers full use of the tenders but only two catamarans were provided to offer this service.

The first one carried 200 passengers and left the ship at 8.15am. There was another one at 8.40am carrying 115 passengers and a third carrying the same amount at 9.45am as they had to allow time for the first catamaran to get back to the ship.

The tours office was offering timed tickets for the boats so a long queue formed from 7am.

I was lucky enough to get a ticket for the 8.40am boat and arranged to meet Ted and Carol on the quay when they came ashore at 9.45am.

I always read my Oriana Today very carefully and I knew I had to wait in the public rooms to hear the announcement to board the ship. But having obtained my ticket early I went out on deck to watch the departing tender and see where it went towards the shore.

Forgetting the time I suddenly discovered it was 8.55am and my boat had not been called. Returning to the tours desk I found I had missed my slot and there was now nothing until the early afternoon as all the earlier catamarans were booked.

Only one dozen tenders were scheduled to take passengers ashore throughout the whole day and soon an angry crowd of people were complaining that they would not have enough time to see the island.

With a 6pm sailing the last tender was due to leave the shore at 5pm and the maximum it could carry was 200 people.

It was not the fault of P&O as the ship to shore disembarkation had been arranged through their agent in Australia but it resulted in chaos in the foyers and a lot of unhappy people sitting around for several hours waiting to go ashore.

My mistake had been cancelling my tour as the excursions went very smoothly and kept to their timings.

Those that went to the Great Barrier Reef came back armed with certificates to prove they had snorkeled amongst the coral. The only drawback was several of them had been very seasick as once outside the harbour it was very rough, especially on the way back.

A few years ago I had suffered panic attacks. I had been a carer for my elderly mother and they stemmed from leaving her for a few hours and returning to find her on the floor as she was unsteady on her feet.

Each time I went out I worried about getting home and this spread into my general life even after her death.

I had fought to control them and this trip on my own was to build up my confidence and get me over this need to be in familiar places.

The ship became my home but in all the other ports I had visited I had been able to walk or take a taxi so returning to Oriana was no problem.

With the chaos caused by the sea trip into Hamilton Island I was struck by a sudden fear. If all the passengers had to wait so long to get on a tender going out, how was I going to get back to the ship in time for sailing?

Suddenly I realized I could not do it and I felt ashamed and angry with myself that I was missing one of the most beautiful islands in the world.

I shut myself in my cabin missing lunch because I did not want to see anyone and explain why I had not gone ashore. Then I found the remotest, highest part of the deserted ship to sit and read my book.

I knew the evening would be the worst when everyone would ask me what I did today and when I walked into my cabin and found Janet sitting there I burst into tears and told her what I had done.

Again I realized how very lucky I was to be sharing a cabin

with her. A total stranger a few weeks ago she had now become my friend and confidante and she convinced me if this was the worst thing that happened in my life I would be very lucky.

I had already made some very good friends on the ship who were looking after me and building up my confidence. Alastair and Nigel from the Food and Beverage Department came and had a drink with me at sailaway and also convinced me that what had happened on day forty-two of my trip did not matter.

"One bad day out of 80 is not bad," they said to me.

In the evening the entertainments department staged a pub night in Harlequins which looked a lot of fun, but by 11pm I was emotionally drained and felt totally exhausted and knew I had to go to bed.

Being on a ship for eighty-days is like living in a community. The huge liner becomes smaller and you make friends and enemies on board.

The difference is you cannot get away and you begin to worry you are getting on people's nerves because you keep bumping into them.

But after the disaster of my first boat port on this cruise I found out the true meaning of friendship and I thanked my lucky stars I was on board.

DAY FORTY THREE
Relaxation and Recovery

The morning after my traumatic experience in the Whitsunday Islands I woke up feeling much more relaxed.

The sun was blazing down from early morning and people were fighting for a space in the shade.

I went to play my usual game of shuffleboard as I felt I might get withdrawal symptoms if I didn't do it!

We reached the semi-finals but after my partner scored two minus tens we were soundly beaten 49 to -6. But it was like a club we had formed on Deck 13 and no-one really minded about winning or losing.

The individual quiz was about jazz and there were very few questions I could answer. I just put Count Basie down several times hoping one of them would be right but in the end his name did not feature in any of the answers.

The afternoon was even hotter and you burnt your feet on the deck by the swimming pool if you did not wear your shoes.

It was another formal night with the Ladies Night Ball and as the female passenger who had bought her white dress in Acapulco was still on board mine remained in the wardrobe.

When I tried it on in the shop I felt like Scarlett O'Hara and was very excited about wearing it on the ship. But one look at this plump little lady in an identical dress put me off mine and I may well end up giving it to a charity shop when I get home.

Chaplin's Cinema was screening the only showing of Wimbledon, a love story between fading British male player Peter Colt and the bad girl of American tennis Lizzie Bradbury, who inspires him to go on and win the coveted Championships.

The story was very far-fetched but the tennis scenes brought back happy memories of the days when I served on the Sussex Lawn Tennis Association Committee and went to Wimbledon every year.

Tennis players played the extras and to make it believable John McEnroe and Chris Evert appeared commentating on Peter's matches.

Former Wimbledon champion Pat Cash was tennis consultant on the film so the tennis scenes were one hundred per cent accurate.

When it finished at midnight I went along to the Pacific Lounge to the late night magical cabaret by Stephen Garcia.

The audience was minimal and he had to work very hard throughout his fast moving show. In the first fifteen minutes we saw more magic than most magicians perform in a forty-five minute show and all his tricks were original.

Stephen was due to give more shows before we reached Hong Kong and I hoped that they would warrant a bigger audience than he had in his Midnight Cabaret.

In the theatre the talented company were once again performing their tribute to Bob Fosse and I would have gone again had I not wanted to see the film.

There are some shows you can watch again and again and most of the musicals presented by the Oriana Theatre Company fell into this category.

The one great advantage of having them on the World Cruise was they were free as all the entertainment is included in your fare.

Had I gone to see Wimbledon at home it would have cost me at least £5 and for the theatre shows which would not disgrace any West End Theatre you would pay upwards of £25.

Many people think a cruise is expensive but if you sit down

and analyse what you get for your money this type of holiday is extremely good value.

I once went on a Roger Taylor Tennis Holiday in Val de Lobo on the Algarve.. It was a package with Silk Cut Holidays in the days when cigarette firms were allowed to sponsor events and vacations.

I was forced to take a single room with a supplement at a hotel because, unlike the ship, they refused to match me up with any other single lady who might want to share.

The tennis coaching with Roger Taylor was free but everything else was extra, including the end of course barbecue which was intended to be a farewell party for the group.

The week's holiday at the Portugese tennis centre cost me twice as much as a fortnight's Meditteranean cruise.

I had worked out that the cost of my 80 day holiday on Oriana was costing very little more than I would have spent back in Britain when you totaled up the cost of heating, light, food, entertainment and travel. Plus rent, council tax and other expenditure.

I can now well understand why elderly people choose to escape the English winter with all the heating bills and live in Spain for three or four months of the year.

DAY FORTY FOUR
Beautifying the Barnet

Forty four days out of Southampton I decided it was time to drastically change my appearance.

With my new-found confidence and my Frank Usher dress I put myself in the hands of the South African hairdresser Lindsey who had cut my hair so beautifully before.

With the hot sun we had been having my hair had gone tortoiseshell from highlights put in my hair six months ago. They were supposed to have been taken out by my hairdresser back home two days before the cruise but they had not done the job properly.

Lindsey took one look at my hair and held up her hands in horror saying she wanted to take it back to its natural colour.

I made an appointment after my tap class and she started work. She selected a deep auburn brown and warned me I would come out looking much darker but I was very pleased with the finished result and it did take years off my age.

I had always shied away from ship's hairdressers believing they were incredibly expensive because they had the monopoly.

Harding Brothers hold the franchise on Oriana and my ninety minute appointment for a full head colour was just £30, far cheaper than you pay at a hairdressers back home.

It was another very hot day on the decks with a warm wind blowing which speeded up our tans. Everyone was now looking a healthy mahogany colour and high factor sun protection cream was being rubbed into exposed flesh at the shuffleboard club.

This time no-one was complaining about the five days at sea because the weather was fine, the sea calm and a lot of people were exhausted after the three Australian ports.

Elaine was getting tough with us at the tap class, teaching us more elaborate steps and making the pace faster.

We were now learning routines to All That Jazz from Chicago and Let's Face the Music and Dance.

Two of us, an American lady called Brenda, and myself had the mad idea of working out our own routine in secret for the last Talent Night of the cruise.

We wanted to do something based on Shirley Temple's

famous performance On The Good Ship Lollipop and dress in gingham dresses with our hair in bunches!

But it all depended on whether we could get a CD of the song in Hong Kong and that was my allocated task.

There was another Fun of the Fair in aid of seamen's charities in the evening and again my skills on the golf putting green was zero. I got one ball in the hole marked two points and five others went all over the Pacific Lounge.

At the other end of the ship Richard Beavis was giving his first performance in the Theatre Royal. Richard has performed all over the world but is best known for his role as Ritchie Vallens in the smash hit Buddy in London's West End.

He gave a polished performance which culminated in the song from Buddy, La Bamba, which brought tumultuous applause.

Two venues on the ship during the World Cruise were not proving as successful as on other cruises I had done.

One was the late night disco in Harlequins and the other was the casino. Despite an excellent DJ Steve Haragan some nights the disco only had two or three people in there, other nights it was really swinging.

In the casino the croupiers stood around night after night

waiting for customers and apart from the first leg the roulette tournaments had to be cancelled due to lack of support.

It was disappointing for me as I enjoy playing roulette and blackjack on cruises as the stakes are relatively low and it is not taken as seriously as the casinos on shore.

Shipboard casinos do attract the serious gamblers but they also welcome the fun punters like myself who bet on a shoestring and give up when they have lost their meagre limit.

Some nights I found myself going to bed far earlier than at home for lack of nightlife on the ship. This is where the World Cruise differs from the shorter two and three week cruises where everyone pushes themselves to the limit every night due to the shorter holidays. Twelve weeks is a long time to live life to the full and I discovered after the first fortnight I had to pace myself to stay the course.

DAY FORTY FIVE
Catwalk debut

Even after forty four days at sea I was always finding new things to do.

On that particular morning I decided to forego my shuffleboard and go to dancing class. The new instructors Michael and Freda Nizinkiewicz, who had joined the ship in Sydney, were due to teach the jive.

Being brought up in the fifties and sixties it was a dance I had always wanted to learn and I found the basic steps very easy. The push turn was the most difficult especially when there were not enough male partners to go round and you had to wait your turn for Michael to dance with you.

Their instructions were clear and precise and it was exhausting, but fun.

In the afternoon it was so hot you burnt your feet on the ground surrounding the swimming pool and it was a welcome relief to slip into the cool water. Healthy tans were now the order of the day, even for those passengers who joined at Sydney, and the smell of coconut from the sun tan lotion pervaded the air.

An exciting evening lay ahead as I was to make my debut as a fashion model wearing my Frank Usher dress.

The Knightsbridge Show of Fashion was to be held twice, at 7.30pm and 9.45pm. I had to be in Harlequins at 7pm for a rehearsal and I was to be escorted by the ship's jeweller Gerard and Robbie from the Casino.

Both of them looked very smart in tuxedos and we were the finale.. It was very exciting to be involved in the show and I had a taste of what it must be like to be a real model.

For the other models, who included the Captain's wife Angie Carr and the Executive Purser's wife it was a mad scramble to make their quick changes behind the scenes.

I remained in my evening dress for the entire show but I felt a bit strange walking through the ship in full evening dress on a casual night.

I decided to change between shows and for the second one I got dressed backstage with the other models instead of in my cabin.

I was sorry when it ended and with it my modeling career. I had a taste for the glamour and bright lights and wished it could continue.

The night was still young and comedian Taffy Spencer was giving another performance, this time in the Pacific Lounge.

He was even funnier than the last time and I thoroughly enjoyed the show.. Sadly he only appeared once more on this short leg of the World Cruise in the Farewell Variety Show.

Tensions were beginning to bubble up in the long-term passengers and the stress of the trip was beginning to set in.

Going down to dinner between shows I was greeted by the lady who had got on in Brisbane "You are not supposed to be here, your place is not laid,." she said.

It was an innocent remark because I had said I might not be down but the culmination of the long time at sea and her words prompted me to make a hasty exit and I sat on deck until it was time for the second show.

Now I was faced with having to eat humble pie the following evening and I tossed and turned all night worrying about it.

DAY FORTY SIX
Highs and Lows

There was no question of my eating humble pie at dinner the next night. I bumped into Ted who told me I had upset them all by over-reacting and he indicated they would rather I did not return.

All the tension of nearly seven weeks at sea came to a head and the floodgates opened. As I was heading back to my cabin I bumped into the female purser Liz who asked me what was wrong.

It was so nice to be able to talk to someone and I told her everything. She said I was to leave it to her and she would get it sorted out. She was as good as her word and when I saw John, the restaurant manager, at the on-deck barbecue at lunchtime he asked me what I would like to do.

I said I was perfectly happy to eat on my own in Al Fresco on deck twelve for the rest of the trip but he would not hear of it.

He suggested I not only change tables but I change restaurants as well so for the remainder of the cruise I would be eating in the Oriental Restaurant in the aft of the ship.

For the second time Oriana was crossing the Equator and for those who had got on the ship in Australia another ceremony was held.

This time I sat nearer the pool and walked around taking photographs instead of sitting high up on the edge of the Jacuzzi above the pool.

I don't know if it was my new position or whether I was in a better frame of mind, but I enjoyed the ceremony far more the second time around.

The whole event was hugely enjoyable and I found myself cheering loudly for King Neptune's team this time instead of P & O. The home team was led this time by Simon the Senior First Officer whilst Neptune was played by the First Officer so when the two of them faced each other on the greasy pole it really was a needle match.

I had to rush off to my tap dancing class afterwards and we were making very good progress. We were now able to do more complicated steps and had learnt a new routine.

I looked forward to the classes which could not happen

every day because we had to alternate with the advanced line dancing.

In the evening I went to meet my new table and found two very nice couples. The third couple on the table, the finance lecturer Richard Allen and his wife, were not down that night.

It was a much easier table as far as conversation went as both couples were younger and more outgoing than my previous table and I hoped this would be my last move.

I decided to attend the Black and White Ball that night and I had dressed for the occasion in the dress I had purchased in Accapulco.

As soon as I put it on I knew I had made a mistake buying it. The huge white lace attachment at the top made me look as if I was a chicken with a doily round its neck.

I went up to the shop and asked them what I could do with this horrible dress. "Put it in the bin." Jane said and I had to agree with her.

I went back to the cabin and changed having decided to assign the dress to the crew bar for when they had a drag night!

There was plenty of dancing and I ended up rocking and

rolling with Richard Beavis, the cabaret artist who played Ritchie Vallens in Buddy.

Dancing with a professional is always good fun and I tried to keep up with his gyrating hips as he swiveled them in perfect time to the rhythm.

I had found all the artists who had appeared on board since Southampton to be very friendly and forthcoming in mixing with the passengers. I had yet to find one who was "starry" and aloof.

I stayed in the disco much later than usual and went to bed after 1am on a high having started the day on a real low.

DAY FORTY SEVEN
Bedside Manners and Mini Skirts

As I approached my half century of days on board Oriana I had a mad idea how to salvage my awful Acapulco dress.

In the evening of the forty-seventh day there was to be another 60s and 70s party night in Harlequins. I had promised the entertainment staff I would enter into the spirit of things this time and dress for the occasion.

Having given up wearing mini skirts some time ago I had not got any with me and the shop had none in stock.

So I took my dress and a pair of scissors and slashed it to bits. I cut off the bodice with the dreadful lace collar, reduced the shirt length by more than half and the result was a full skirt that came four inches above my knees.

Janet begged me not to bend down or I would give all the old men on board a heart attack but I teamed it up with shiny black tights, a close fitting black velvet bodice and high heeled black ankle boots.

I bought a belt from the shop and I felt the bees knees as I tried on the costume. To finish the effect I added my Elton John star-shaped sun glassed with pink lenses and a glittery frame made up of the American flag. I had bought them in San Francisco for a bit of fun, now was my chance to show them off to their full effect.

I spent the day doing the usual routine looking forward to the evening when I could make a real fool of myself at the party.

At 6.30pm the four actors plus a young man from the Oriana Theatre Company performed their second production, Bedside Manners by Derek Benfield.

Having enjoyed Don't Dress For Dinner so much I went full of high expectations. But I found the play was not as good as the previous one.

Robert Duncan was excellent in the lead role and the others were also very good in their parts but it was old-fashioned farce in the Brian Rix style, all dropping trousers and rushing in and out of opposing doors.

I had been brought up on the Whitehall farces as my parents loved them but I had found them boring and I can't remember laughing much at any of them. I used to sit there as guffaws surrounded me wondering why the audience found them so funny.

Don't Dress For Dinner had been more of a slick comedy than a farce and that is why I enjoyed it so much. Having made friends with the cast who were sadly leaving us in Hong Kong I was disappointed that I had not enjoyed their final production as much as I would have liked.

I got some strange looks as I went down to dinner in my sixties gear – minus the glasses – but as soon as I got into Harlequins I was joined by weird and wonderful outfits worn by the entertainment officers which really took me back to my youth.

Powerhouse was providing the music, interspersed with 60s CDs and the floor was full of dancers from fifteen to eighty five. There was a wonderful old lady twisting away on the dance floor oblivious to the fact she had no partner. She was really enjoying herself and hardly left the floor.

I was exhausted having gyrated my way through every dance from 9.45pm to midnight and I began to wonder if I was getting too old for such heated activity.

It was one of the "great nights" on Oriana and I hoped that we would have another one before we finally reached

Amanda Wilkins

Southampton.

Despite having another five weeks to go my thoughts were beginning to turn to home and I knew I had to start thinking about what I was going to do and where I was going to live when I got back.

This trip had changed me in several ways. In Australia I had felt happier than I had done for many months and now I was gaining confidence and feeling more self-assured. The world was my oyster and the cruise had made me realize it was a very small place.

DAY FORTY EIGHT
KOTA KINABALU

When I booked the World Cruise I had no idea where this place with the unpronounceable name was, then someone told me it is the new name for Borneo.

It lies on the west coast of Sabah, one of the two states of East Malaysia, and is the capital of one of the most dynamic and flourishing towns in Borneo.

The approach was very picturesque and we could see it was an easy walk into the town, even though the ship was providing shuttle buses.

I had debated whether to take an excursion on a train into the mangrove plantations and visit a beach, then I decided I would like to walk into the town and beyond having been on the ship for five days without seeing land.

It was a very pretty walk and Sabah, , which is surrounded on three sides by sea, is unspoilt by tourism as it is only in recent years visitors have discovered the virgin charms of the world's third largest island, Borneo and particularly the northern territory.

Just north of the Equator the weather was hot although there was a short, sharp shower of rain as I neared the town.

It is a Muslim country and we were asked to respect their traditions. They expect their women to be covered as much as possible and I saw several ladies in long dresses with their heads covered..

I wore a long sleeved cotton shirt and cropped trousers and although I was very hot I felt comfortable amongst the locals and did not receive any disapproving looks.

From the shore I could clearly see the longhouses built on stilts where the Muruts live. They cling to their past more than any of the other tribes as they are more remote from modern civilization.

Thirty or more families live in each longhouse and they retain their love of traditional songs and dance.

As we sailed into the port the local band was playing for us with some of the most beautiful women in the world dressed in national costume handing us beads of welcome.

Musician on quay in Kota Kinabalu

On the quay I watched the Bajaus fishermen preparing their nets and going out in their boats. The most numerous ethnic group in Sabah are the Kadazans who live mostly in the coastal areas and grow rice and trading for a living.

It was very strange to arrive in the centre of town and see familiar names like The Body Shop, KFC and McDonalds and I came across an old man begging playing his violin for money.

As he sat cross-legged on the pavement the most beautiful music came from his instrument and it seemed incongruous in such a setting.

An artist was displaying his paintings and I was drawn to a small picture of an orangutan which I bought from him for 20 Malaysian Ringgits.

It was in the huge shopping mall I had my biggest surprise. There were so many contact lens centres, every other shop was selling them and spectacles. There were also a lot of mobile phone shops.

Town center Kota Kinabalu

One passenger went in and had her eyes tested only to come away with two pairs of glasses for the equivalent of £90.

Everything was very cheap and I bought four pairs of shoes for fifty ringgits (approximately £7.50) each.

I got two pairs of handmade sandals with painted wooden soles, a pair of gold evening mules and a pair of lilac mules. The difficulty I had was finding the shoe shops that had my shoes to fit my size eight feet as the Malaysians are all extremely tiny.

It was the same in the clothes shops as their large size is the equivalent to our small or medium. But tucked away on the top floor amid the restaurants I found a shop selloing nothing but evening dresses.

I tried on two wine coloured velvet gowns and bought one for two hundred ringgits. Arriving back at the ship I discovered I had paid £30 for a dress that on the ship would have cost me £300 so I went back on the shuttle bus after lunch and bought the other one.

As we sailed out of Kota Kinabalu at 6pm I watched the sun go down and saw the most beautiful sunset I had seen the whole trip.

It was a humid but fine evening for the Cruise Director's

last Hoedown on deck. Christine Noble was leaving us in Hong Kong and all her line dancers came along to support her last event.

Exhausted from the day I fell into bed but I was exhilherated from my first visit to Malaysia and pursuing one of my favourite hobbies – shopping.

DAY FORTY NINE
Dining under the Stars

Forty nine days at sea put us near Hong Kong and England seemed a very long way away. In the morning paper I saw they were having a cold snap and snow was expected as we were basking in the sunshine.

Having bought so much the previous day I was delighted when the purser's office informed us that a bin was being put in the foyer to receive clothing contributions for the Tsunami Relief Fund.

I had a blitz on my wardrobe and decided to part with my thickest clothes. Arriving back in England on Easter Tuesday at the end of March I couldn't believe it would be cold enough for fur jackets and thick skirts. This would relieve my suitcase considerably.

With Hong Kong just two days away I knew I would shop till I dropped there as that is what the city is famous for.

Nigel had promised to take me to dine under the stars on the top deck and carried away by the atmosphere I was hoping for a touch of romance. I built up the "date" to be something really special and I had my hair done in the morning. I decided after lunch to have a sleep after lunch so I could sparkle in the evening..

I went to bed at 12 noon and at 1pm Janet came in not knowing I was there. I looked up and said "Good Morning" so I must have been well away!

I slept till 3pm and felt revived and ready for my evening. As it was a formal night, I decided to wear one of my new Malaysian dresses and I was very pleased with the purchase. This was the night I had been looking forward to since we first arranged it.

Up to now I had only spent about fifteen minutes with Nigel each evening in the bar, now we were going to spend the whole evening together.

We had arranged to meet in the Crow's Nest for a pre-dinner drink and he was there when I arrived, "Here's your drink," he said "I forgot the Masons. Wait here and I'll be back after the speeches"

Not a good start to my romantic evening. When the dinner gong went and I was left in a deserted bar I was getting really irritated. I asked the barman to send Nigel a message and ask if I should go down to dinner as usual. The barman told me he was very busy and I shouldn't wait but I wasn't going to miss my al fresco meal.

When Nigel arrived he was not in the best of moods and we walked through to our table on the open deck. With a candle in the middle and a huge full moon surrounded by a ring of light it was the perfect setting, but neither of us felt very sociable.

The menu in the Terrace Grill is more extensive than in the restaurants and the atmosphere is more like a very expensive, exclusive restaurant.

Nigel had mixed grill and I had a steak so large I could not eat it all. We were looked after very well, but from the beginning the evening had turned sour and we were both in a bad mood. So much so I found Nigel the following day and asked if we could do it again. Expecting him to turn me down I was pleased he agreed to give it another go..

After dinner we went to watch the third version of The Weakest Link, Don't Break The Chain.

This time the team included the Staff Captain Charlie Carr and the Executive Purser Zak Coombs. I was rooting for them to be in the final but it was won by the port presenter Kirsty Brook. This one was back to the standard of the first one I had seen and was hugely enjoyable.

As I was about to go to bed I was joined by the actors and their respective partners who invited me to join them for dinner at their table the following night. Their time on board had gone extremely quickly and I was going to miss them when they got off in Hong Kong.

It was one of the latest nights I had stayed up on the whole cruise as I eventually got to bed at 1.30am. For the first time I woke Janet up and she said she wouldn't allow me to sleep in the afternoon again.

It was amazing that after forty-nine nights sharing a small cabin we had never had a serious argument or wanted to change cabins. I had heard some horrendous tales of strangers sharing who hated each other from the word go. But because the ship was so full they were stuck with each other for the duration.

We were lucky to have an outside cabin as it made it seem bigger. Had we been in an inside two-bedded cabin it would have seemed more claustrophobic and may well have led to us getting on each other's nerves.

Janet is a remarkable person and I hoped she would keep in touch with me when the cruise ended.

DAY FIFTY
The Last Supper

Although it was a very hot day and I was having fun I was hit by a terrible bout of homesickness on the day I clocked up my half century at sea.

I almost wished I was going home from Hong Kong even though we had some of the best ports to come.

I didn't know why I felt like that but I had been warned there would be a stage when I would go through it.

The actors and their respective partners had all become good friends and I was very sad they were flying home from Hong Kong. I had spent a lot of time in their company since their play had been performed and I would miss them all.

In the afternoon I joined Fraser Hines, Vicki Michelle and her daughter Louise in the cricket nets to play the first game of the cruise.

I had been threatening to play since the first leg but Charlie, the horse racing addict who was at our table on the first leg was an ardent cricketer. He told me I was being selfish as cricket was a man's game and women shouldn't play!

Now several women passengers played and I was one of four in our team. Each batsman plays two overs and if you are out during that time you lose five points each time.

I went down to minus ten but then got used to the bowling and brought my score back up again to plus four. My bowling was not too bad either but I knew I had to improve my fielding as I dropped two catches.

I found it tremendous fun and more exhilarating than shuffleboard and I decided this would be my afternoon activity until we reached Southampton.

As it was the last day of this leg of the cruise the Snowball Jackpot Bingo had to be won and there was £1400 on offer. That would pay my rent for three months when I got back and I spent £10 on three books of bingo tickets.

The nearest I got to winning anything was needing one number to win £30. As I had played on and off since Southampton I think I must accept that I am a born loser as far as bingo is concerned.

Fraser Hines approached me on behalf of the company to

invite me to join their table for dinner as it was their last night.

A quick trip down to the Oriental Restaurant to apologise to my table and it was all sorted. We met in the Crow's Nest for a pre-dinner drink and then went down for our meal in the Peninsular Restaurant.

Sue Hodge and her husband were on first sitting so I sat with Robert Duncan and his wife Jean, Fraser Hines, Vicki Michelle and her husband Graham and fifteen year old daughter Lou.

Vicki Michelle from Allo Allo

It was a very pleasant and relaxed evening, a marked contrast to the previous night, and by the end I had recovered my equilibrium.

We went to see Chiefly Yourselves, the talent show that I took part in last leg. Elaine had decided we had done our showcase, now we had to perfect our new tap routine before we would perform in public again.

Robert Duncan (Drop the Dead Donkey) and Frazer Hines (Emmerdale)

One act that will remain in my memory forever was Grant, a giant of a man from Brisbane who got up and sang Pretty Woman very flat. Robert decided to call for an encore and he did it all over again before starting on I Call Australia Home.

He was even worse in that song, so much so a lady from the audience got up to help him out. But you had to admire his courage for getting up to do it. The man sitting in front of us turned to Robert and said, "Don't you dare call for another encore!"

I went to bed after I watched my actor friends do the walk down and take their final bows in the Farewell Concert.

It is always sad to see the end of a leg of the World Cruise but it is also quite exciting as a new chapter was about to begin.

DAY FIFTY ONE
HONG KONG

I never thought that I would ever be fed up with shops, but after visiting the terminal building at Ocean Terminal in Hong Kong I felt I never wanted to see another shop again.

It is supposed to be the best port terminal in the world with over two hundred shops on three floors. But as most of them are the top designers the prices were well above my range and it was so vast I could never find my way back to the ship.

Four times I went through the terminal and each time I got lost. I found very few people spoke English and it was all a bit overwhelming.

We docked in Kowloon at 8am on a misty, rainy day. You could not see the top of the massive skyscrapers or the famous Victoria Peak. From the top you should get a 360 degree panoramic view of Hong Kong Island, Kowloon and the New Territories.

I planned to go ashore as soon as possible and take the Star Ferry across to Hong Kong Island where I could get the Peak Tram to the top. This is the steepest funicular railway in the world and it has been running since 1888.

But seeing the weather I abandoned that idea and decided to walk around the town. Our berth in Ocean Terminal was in the heart of Kowloon and I only had to walk through the vast shopping mall to reach the hub.

This was my first visit to Hong Kong and when I went out into the streets I found it all a bit scary to start with. I had never seen so many people, traffic and skyscrapers. Again I found many people spoke no English and if you asked them a question they shrugged their shoulders.

I wanted to get a jade bangle and I went in search of the jade shops. The first one I went to wanted twelve thousand Hong Kong dollars, which was very expensive and far more than I could afford.

I then found a small shop where the Chinese lady sold me a bright green bangle for one thousand HK dollars. She told me it was new jade and was not very good but good for the price.

Looking for presents to take back home I went into an antique and gift shop and the assistant looked at my bracelet in horror. She asked me where I got it and told me it was not jade, it was far too green.

I decided to return to the original shop and confront the woman who had sold it to me as I wanted the genuine article. When she immediately returned my money I knew I had been duped and I went back to the second shop where I bought a natural jade bangle in pale green.

Several years ago a close friend of mine had bought me back a fake Rolex from New York. It looked exactly like the real thing and lasted two years and I knew they were available in Hong Kong if you looked for them.

In retrospect what I did was very silly but the new-found confidence I had built up on this cruise had left me with no fear.

I left the main road and walked up a side street, one side of which was lined with blue portaloos.

I passed the flower and fruit markets before I found what I was looking for. A furtive watch dealer selling from a small booth. "Have you got a Rolex?" I asked and he disappeared into the back of the shop returning with a screwed up bit of paper.

He produced a man's watch exactly like the expensive Rolex watches I had seen advertised. I asked him if he could make the strap smaller and he agreed. As he searched for his tools in his drawer all the time he looked like a frightened rabbit, keeping his eyes glued to the street outside.

Eventually he said he could not serve me as he had not got a small screw so I carried on up the road until I found another watch dealer. I asked the same question and he asked if it was for a lady or a gentleman.

When I told him it was for me he produced a smaller version which fitted perfectly. He set the time and date for me and I handed over five hundred Hong Kong dollars, about thirty English pounds.

HONG KONG

Amanda Wilkins

He asked me to wear it and when I said I would prefer to take it back to the ship he gave me a pink satin bag and told me to keep it hidden in the bottom of my bag till I got on board.

I decided not to go back to the ship for lunch and I found a genuine Chinese Sushi Bar in the basement of a shopping mall.

We sat round a conveyor belt that carried the plates of sushi round in various price ranges and you lifted off your selection. With it you got a mug of china tea which you filled from a tap in front of you.

This was not a tourist attraction, it was filled with Chinese businessmen and mothers with children as it is as popular with them as McDonalds is with English kids.

They were all laughing at me because I did not know how to use chopsticks and a very nice Chinese lady who was with her daughter gave me a lesson.

I was just returning to the ship about 3pm when I heard a band and going round the corner I came across the magnificent Lion Dance. I had seen it on the television but never live. After gyrating on the ground the front man in the lion suit climbed up a tall pole and performed the dance high in the air.

The famous Dragon Dance

In the evening Janet and I went on the Evening Harbour Cruise. We were bussed to Hong Kong Island where we joined our Chinese junk. We cruised slowly out to the Easttern Harbour passing the tall buildings which make up the main banking and commercial area of Hong Kong.

There was a laser show from the roofs of several buildings in the harbour and the guide pointed out the HSBC headquarters and the international finance centre, the tallest building in Hong Kong.

I was brought up on Richard Mason's book The World of Suzy Wong and I was delighted when the boat took us past Wan Chai, where the story was set. Now it has evolved into a prominent commercial district adorned with giant neon signs along the rooftops and harbour front buildings.

We also passed the protruding runway of the former international airport Kai Tak which is now a golf driving range.

We arrived back at the ship at 10pm, just in time to see the most wonderful folkloric performance by a local dance group.

They performed another version of the lion dance with one big and two small lions and then the girls gave us a fan dance before the acrobats came on. The climax was a strange dance when the leader changed the colour of his face mask before our eyes with no visible means of doing it.

A lot of us decided to stay up until 1am to see us sail out of Hong Kong and many of the buildings were still lit up. Long after I retired to my cabin I watched the lights of the city fading into the distance through my window.

It is not a place where I would like to live and work as it is too crowded for me and there is too much hustle and bustle. But I am so glad I have had the opportunity to see it and I certainly enjoyed the visit.

DAY FIFTY-TWO
Homesickness and Depression

This was one of those depressing days when the weather slipped back to winter. It was grey and overcast with constant rain showers. It made me think more of an Autumn day at home than a sunshine cruise halfway round the world.

I went to the port lecture on Vietnam and then went to the travelling alone get-together to see an old friend Ian Fraser who had just taken over from Christine Noble as cruise director.

It was a strange day when my thoughts turned to home and although I had enjoyed the cruise I was now looking forward to returning to Newhaven.

I played cricket in the rain in the afternoon as I had now become a regular part of the team. It was fun to take part but it would have been better for all of us if the weather had not been so inclement.

My homesickness increased during the afternoon and I decided to telephone my business partner Chris Morgan. It was just after 9am in England and I knew he would be at home.

He seemed pleased to hear me and we chatted for quite a long time irrespective of my bill. Talking to him cheered me up and I looked forward to the evening ahead.

It was the fourth Captain's Welcome Aboard party of the cruise and I decided to go to the Crow's Nest even though I had changed my table from the Peninsular to the Oriental restaurant. After a quick drink there I went to the Pacific Lounge where my restaurant was supposed to go.

I found I did not enjoy that party as much as I did not know anyone in the room except the officers and I decided in future to stick to the Crow's Nest.

I wore my tight Chinese dress I had bought in Hong Kong which was marked XXL (extra extra large) and I could understand why the street girls in Suzy Wong's time all stood at the bar – it was impossible to sit down!

After dinner I went to the Welcome Aboard Ball for a lively evening of dancing before retiring to bed in preparation for Vietnam.

DAY FIFTY THREE
VIETNAM

This was one of the most interesting ports on the whole cruise. As a teenager I lived with stories about the Vietnam War and although Great Britain was not involved it was widely reported in the British papers.

Vietnam

It began in 1954 and did not end until 1975. The Communist influence in South Vietnam had been driven underground in the late 1950s but troops (the Viet Cong) from the north began to take a more active part in the south.

Many villagers were converted to the Communist cause and at first the United States of America was only involved in an advisory capacity and in arming and training the Vietnamese army.

In March 1965 US marines landed in Da Nang and within three years there were 500,000 American troops in Vietnam. A long bombing campaign began in March 1965 and more bombs were dropped in North Vietnam than were used in the whole of World War Two.

The bombing campaign (Operation Rolling Thunder) was not a success and by 1967 world opinion was against American involvement and the war was also becoming increasingly unpopular in America.

The last American troops left Vietnam almost exactly eight years after the marines landed at Da Nang. The war continued until April 30 1975 when a T-54 tank smashed through the gates of the Presidential Palace at Saigon (now called Ho Chi Min City). A month earlier Da Nang had fallen to the Viet Cong.

The Socialist Republic of Vietnam is a long and often very narrow country bordered to the north by China and to the west by Laos and Cambodia. Vietnam is still a relatively poor country and tourism is still in its infancy.

Vietnam is one of the few remaining Communist countries in the world and it is very noticeable. We docked at Tiensa, about ten miles from Da Nang and police were on the quay all day watching people on the stalls and when I said I would like to go for a walk and take some photographs I was told very firmly I was not allowed through the dock gates on foot, I had to choose the shuttle bus.

Although from the deck of the ship I could see quite a pretty walk I was also told there was nothing to see and I had to remain in the dock area.

In the morning I took an excursion to the Cham Museum , Da Nang's main attraction. A u-shaped building around a central courtyard it contains the biggest and best display of Cham art in the world.

After a leisurely stroll around the museum I picked up a trishaw for a tour of the city and this was one of the most terrifying experiences of my life.

80 Days at Sea

The cyclist pushing me from behind seemed oblivious to the traffic coming at us from all directions and I felt I was escaping death my seconds.

A Trader on the quay at Da Nang

Every twist and turn may have rewarded me with the sights and sounds of this bustling city but to me it was hell on earth and not something I will ever do again. Half way through my tour my "driver" decided to do a u-turn in the middle of the traffic.Ignoring the blaring car horns he swung me round to go back the way we had come.

We passed by the Han river before stopping at the open market and if I could have picked up a taxi back to the ship from there I would have done.

After a visit to a local embroidery workshop we eventually reached the safety of our coach back at the Cham Museum.

After a couple of Pimms number one on board to calm my nerves I decided to venture ashore again to do my shopping on the quay.

It was there I picked up all my presents to take home as things were remarkably cheap. Silk ties for three dollars each, marble boxes and mirrors inlaid in beautiful wooden cases.

I also picked up a marble budha and two green marble dragons for myself. How I would get off the ship in Southampton in a month's time was something I would have to work out. The weather had remained dull all day and it was cold as we set sail for Singapore at 6pm. Each leg of the cruise had bought us more fascinating ports and this was certainly one of the most interesting.

DAY FIFTY FOUR
Back to the Sunshine

On the morning after Vietnam when it had been cold and windy we woke to find the sun blazing down and another very hot day.

So hot it burnt your feet as you walked round the pool and with the return of the sunsine so the smiles returned to people's faces.

Passengers, some tanned almost black, stretched out on the sun loungers in the briefest of bikinis and swimming trunks and the shuffleboarders dropped their paddles because their hands were covered in sun tan lotion.

I survived the first round then crashed out in the second so I went along to the short tennis competition and where I lost in the first round.

Completing the hat trick I went down to the pool where I lost the individual quiz on chocolates and sweets.

I had become good friends with the pursers in the food and

beverage department and I met Nigel and Carl Luxford for lunch on deck. They worked very hard so it was a rare treat to be able to sit down with them on a social occasion.

Our lunch over-ran so I missed my cricket but as I had not scored a single run at my last attempt perhaps this was a good thing.

We had our tap class at 4pm and we were learning more and more steps. I knew I had to keep on with this back on land as I had worked so hard and progressed so far. It is good exercise and I found it hugely enjoyable, more so than line dancing which I found very repetitive.

The evening's entertainment included another round of Call My Bluff and Elizabeth Leggett who I had joined at the first one caught my arm as I walked along the deck.

"Les has been ill for four days," she said. "I am too upset to talk about it but I am on my own tonight so you will join me, won't you?"

After dinner I kept my word and went to find her in the Pacific lounge. The panel was the same, Angie Carr the Captain's wife, staff captain Charlie Carr (no relation to the Captain) and Simon the tours manager.

Another couple joined us at the table but we did not do so well. We missed Les, who had been the star of the last team and knew everything.

I had cruised with P & O since I was seventeen but I found this World Cruise very strange. After 11pm the ship was virtually empty and the casino, disco and bars were deserted.

I went up to the Crow's Nest to hear Powerhouse jazzing it up but sadly there were very few people listening to them.

I hoped that on the last leg, with two weeks to go, the ship would liven up a bit at night as we were nearing home. I desperately wanted to go home with happy memories but I found I was now longing to get off the ship for good.

DAY FIFTY FIVE
Sport to the Fore

This was the day I was at my most sporting. I played shuffleboard in the morning and finished at 11.45am. I had made an appointment with Nigel to book a party I wanted to throw for all the people who had been so kind to me.

The problem was there was no 12 noon. Because we had to insert a time change before Singapore the clocks went forward at that time..

This caused chaos throughout the ship because the Conservatory was used to people staggering their lunches, some going at 12 and some at 1pm. When 12 noon became 1pm everyone descended on the place at the same time.

It also caused problems with my schedule. By the time I had finished my business with Nigel it was 1.30pm and I was playing cricket at 2pm.

A hasty lunch was followed by a dash to the cabin to get my correct shoes and a mad dash back up to deck thirteen.

I excelled in my batting getting caught out four times and

scoring minus twenty in two overs. I did make up for it in my bowling taking a wicket and preventing the batsman from getting many runs in my allocated twelve balls.

For the first time since I had started playing I was on the winning team and it felt very good.

Elated by my success I decided to stay on the deck to play short tennis despite the blazing heat so I eventually went down to change for dinner having played sport for five hours.

I had just achieved sapphire status in the P & O's new supporters club, the Portunis and I had been invited to my first party that night. I had already received my free gift of a chrome cruet set in the shape of a ship.

The party was very similar to the Captain's welcome aboard parties and after a couple of drinks I was ready to go down to dinner.

It was a quiet night on board as the passengers were preparing for two ports on subsequent days, Singapore and Kuala Lumpur so I just met Lindsey my South African hairdresser for a drink and had a few dances in Harlequins.

I was finding about 5pm each day now my thoughts were turning to home and I remembered Newhaven Royal British Legion was holding its monthly meeting that night. I sent an email to them saying I was thinking of them and looking forward to returning home.

It had been a very enjoyable cruise and a great experience but after nearly sixty days at sea I was ready to return to the UK. But not too soon as parts of the South East had been brought to a standstill by blizzards and the worst affected areas were the North and South Downs in Sussex and Kent.

DAY FIFTY SIX
SINGAPORE

I got up early to see us arrive in the city of colours, cultures, cuisine and contrasts.

We were in the container berth about forty minutes from the town and I decided to take a taxi instead of queueing for the shuttle bus.

I hired a driver for two hours for eighty Singapore dollars (about £25) and he took me first to Chinatown in South Bridge Road.

This was still decorated for the Chinese New Year and the bustling, busy sections of the town is one of the most popular attractions in Singapore.

My taxi driver, who would keep calling me Annabelle, took me first to a jewellery workshop where I bought a string of seed pearls for fifty Singapore dollars.

We then went to a camera shop where I decided to upgrade my digital camera and I purchased a tiny Ranger for three hundred and fifty Singapore dollars (one hundred pounds).

I declined to buy anything at the silk shop as I had bought

enough silk items in Vietnam so it was on to the Sultan's Mosque in Arab Street which is a focal point for Muslim Singapore.

It makes a stunning landmark of the area with its huge gold dome. The original mosque which stood on the site in North Bridge Road was built with the help of a grant from Sir Stamford Raffles. The present one was completed in 1928.

No-one can visit Singapore without going to the world-famous Raffles Hotel. Somerset Maugham once called it the legendary symbol for "all the fables of the Exotic East." Few hotels can look back on more than a century of legendary service to so many distinguished guests and fewer still have preserved their past with a more loving attention to detail.

Raffles Hotel, Singapore

Raffles Hotel was established in 1887 and designated as a National Monument one hundred years later. It closed in March 1989 for major restoration and re-opened in September 1991.

In the 1920s and 1930s the hotel was a mecca for celebrities such as Charlie Chaplin, Mary Pickford, Douglas Fairbanks, Somerset Maugham and Noel Coward as well as for sultans and statesmen.

I wandered round the leafy terraces and visited the gift shop to get my statutory souvenirs before going to the Long Bar for a Singapore Sling. This is the only bar in the world where you eat the peanuts and throw the shells on the floor.

As I made my way back to the front I asked the uniformed doorman if I could look inside. As I was respectably dressed I was allowed into the hallowed lobby usually reserved for residents.

I stared in awe at the grand timber staircase and the soaring atrium.I could feel a real sense of history as I followed in the footsteps of royalty and film stars.

Raffles is an oasis amidst the city skyscrapers of contemporary Singapore. But the city is so clean with wide streets and trees lining the motorway out of town.

Amanda Wilkins

Raffles Hotel and the author with the doorman

80 Days at Sea

It lacked the hustle and bustle of Hong Kong and although the traffic was heavy my taxi driver told me they never had jams, it always keeps moving.

The city is clean because anyone caught throwing litter anywhere faces a fine of up to one thousand Singapore dollars. Repeat offenders are fined up to two thousand Singapore dollars and also face a corrective work order, cleaning up public places.

This was one of my most favourite ports of call and the taxi ride was the best eighty dollars I had ever spent.

As we were in port again the following day I decided to cut out all entertainment in the evening and went to bed straight after dinner.

DAY FIFTY SEVEN
PORT KELANG

This was the port for Kuala Lumpur in Malaysia but as it was twenty five miles from the city the ship was not running a shuttle bus.

The alternatives were to take a tour or pay £24 to go by bus, spend the day exploring on your own and catch the bus back at the end of the day. The journey into town took just over an hour and with the temperatures in the nineties I decided not to make the journey.

The terminal at Port Kelang (Klang) is one of the most beautiful buildings in the world. With a long walkway from the ship to the terminal it has an attractive red roof and three floors of shops.

Port Kelang is on the west coast of Peninsular Malaysia in the state of Selangor and is a very pretty little place. After looking at the shops and getting a few presents I decided to take a walk.

It was the first time for ages I had trodden on grass

underneath the palm trees. I walked to the outskirts of the port which gave me a splendid view back towards the terminal and the ship.

Bushes of colourful flowers were in abundance and it was definitely my kind of place, wild and remote with nothing but a few houses and the mangrove swamps which are a nature reserve for the snakes.

I walked for most of the morning despire the heat before returning to a near-deserted ship for lunch with Nigel and Carl from the purser's department.

They were having a much easier day than they did in Singapore when they spent the whole day in blazing sunshine supervising the loading of the stores on to the ship.

I went ashore for another short walk in the afternoon before the coaches from Kuala Lumpur carrying exhausted passengers arrived back at the ship. Whilst they looked wilted from their sightseeing and shopping I felt refreshed and happy from my day in the port.

Whether it was the length of the cruise causing tension or just that some passengers are naturally rude but for the first time on the entire trip I experienced the unfr4iendliness of some people that evening.

After buying myself a drink at the bar in the Crow's Nest I approached a group I knew by sight as they had been on since Southampton.

Explaining I was on my own I asked if it was all right to join them until dinner time. One of the group turned to me and told me it was not all right and didn't I know it was very rude to try and muscle in on someone else's group.

Feeling shell-shocked I left my drink and the bar but luckily these incidents were very rare and most of my fellow passengers were extremely friendly.

I was delighted that singer Denise Nolan had joined the ship in Singapore for five days as I had seen her in my favourite musical Blood Brothers.

She was giving two shows, the first of which was the night we left Port Kelang. Even though she must have been jet lagged from her trip she gave a splendid performance and it was not surprising she received rapturous applause

DAY FIFTY EIGHT
An Irish Coleen

This was a red-letter day in my sporting calendar. At cricket I scored thirteen runs with no minuses for being out and I clean bowled one of the opposition, middle stump.

I had dropped a note to Denise Nolan after her show to ask if I could talk to her about her career and I got a very sweet reply inviting me to meet her in Andersons Bar at 9.30pm. It meant coming out of dinner early but I wasn't going to refuse.

The author with Denise Nolan

She was already there when I arrived with her partner of thirty years Tom Anderson, and she told me she had lived with music all her life.

Her mother, Maureen Breslin, had gone to the Irish Academy of Music when she was seventeen which was a remarkable achievement as most of her fellow students were in their thirties.

Denise's mother had become the Irish Forces Sweetheart and her father Tommy Nolan was the Irish Frank Sinatra.

"My dad died the same year has his hero Frank Sinatra, 1998," Denise said. "He simply worshipped him."

Tommy and Maureen had eight children, Linda, Bernadette, Coleen, Brian, Maureen, Denise, Anne and Tommy.

Originally they were the Irish equivalent of the Von Trapp family as all ten of them sang together.

"Coleen was three when we started," she said. "We called ourselves The Singing Nolans."

The family had emigrated to Blackpool from Dublin and when they were offered a contract in London the boys did not want to leave Blackpool.

"Our agent said the six girls would be more marketable so Mum and Dad were happy to drop out of the act," Denise said.

Their first big break came in a television series with Cliff Richard and they did Junior Showtime with Jess Yates.

When Denise's sisters decided they wanted to join the pop music scene Denise decided to leave the act.

"I didn't want to be a pop singer and I thought if I don't do it now I never would," she said.

She left the act in 1978 but she said it was all very amicable. "Families tend to fall out more than strangers," she said. "But you blow up and the next day it is all forgotten."

Gradually the act became fewer when Anne left to have a baby and then Linda left but Anne returned and she and Maureen still go out as the Nolans.

"Maureen has been asked to audition for Blood Brothers and if she gets it Anne will just do her own thing.

"They'll have to call it Blood Sisters soon if Maureen goes into it," she said. "Linda's still playing Mrs Johnson in the show in the West End then going out on tour, Bernie's done the same part and I played it for a year in London and two years on tour."

Denise first met Tom at the New London Theatre where the Nolans were discovered. He was playing the drums in O'Haras

Showband and now he travels with her playing the drums and supporting ninety per cent of the time.

She has done cruising for years and loves seeing the world. "It is very easy work," she said. "But sometimes the audience is difficult. You are living with them and if they hate your show you see them every day."

Denise said she was terrified when she first left her sisters. "The Nolans were very big and when I left the act they were becoming very big on the pop scene. I got in a big panic trying to put together a top class solo act.

"The hardest thing about doing a show is talking to the audience. It is very important you talk to them between songs and that is not easy."

Denise has now established herself as a first rate solo artist and after the cruise she was going on to do a tour she has put together herself about Judy Garland.

We sat talking for over an hour before going out on deck to watch the Mardi Gras show staged by Oriana Theatre Company.

The ship had dropped anchor off Phucket at 9.30pm so it was very calm and warm. Denise and Tom stayed and talked to passengers until the evening ended at 1am and she wowed everyone with her Irish charm

DAY FIFTY NINE
PHUKET

This was one of the saddest ports of call on the whole trip. I had always dreamed of going to Thailand and the pictures I had seen of Phuket made it seem the most beautiful place in the world.

Having planned my voyage in July 2004 I sat glued to my television screen on Boxing Day transfixed by the scenes of horror that was unfolding before my eyes.

We sailed from Southampton on January 7th and were due to visit Phuket on March 7th. When we left the UK we had no idea whether it would still be on the itinerary and it was not until mid February Captain Carr announced the Health Authorities had given the all-clear us to call there.

We had to go ashore by the ship's lifeboats and local tenders. Embarkation was a bit late due to the wind gusting at 50 mph which made it very difficult for the lifeboats to come alongside.

The Captain had a difficult decision to make. Should he allow the passengers to go or disappoint many people by aborting the whole operation. In the end the wind dropped slightly and he decided to carry on with the disembarkation.

I was allocated a ticket for one of the lifeboats and it was certainly a bumpy ride in. We had all the flaps down to prevent us getting wet so we could not see where we were going.

One of the passengers started singing Yellow Submarine and it was a fun twenty minute crossing. Afterwards complaints were made to the purser's office about the short trip. Some passengers felt we should have made the crossing in silence as a mark of respect..

As we approached the shore I saw the sandbags that were supporting the temporary pontoon – the landing stage had been washed away on December 27th..

We landed on the most beautiful beach I have ever seen. More than two miles of soft golden sand fringed with palm trees. I kicked off my sandals and walked along the edge of the warm water letting the sand sift between my toes.

This was the beach where the tsunami had hit and I stood looking out to sea trying to imagine what it must have been like on that fateful day..

Colourful stalls lined the edge of the beach selling Thai

silk garments at incredibly cheap prices. Without exception the passengers all spent more than they intended to try and help these charming, friendly people.

The beach at Phuket

After being on the beach for about an hour in stifling heat I decided to explore the town and I went to cross the main road, totally unaware of the scene of utter destruction that was about to face me.

Where once luxurious hotels had stood there was now just rubble. A broken sign offering food and drink lay on on top of a pile of rocks.

The Tsunami damage at Phuket

The heart had been ripped out of nearly every building facing the beach and although some work has started to put right the damage caused by the cruel sea it will take years before they are fully restored.

Some places will never be rebuilt as they don't have the money. I learnt afterwards that the Thai Government had turned down all offers of monetary help. The passengers had been asked to donate clothes to help the tsunami victims but when we arrived in Phuket the Thai Authorities refused to accept them. Instead they were welcomed with open arms in our next port of call Colombo.

The Tsunami damage at Phuket

I had intended to spend the whole day on the beach but what I had seen upset me so much I caught the local tender back to the ship at lunchtime. I sat on the open deck reflecting on the disaster that had occurred just two months before.

Terrorism you can fight but you have no control over the weather and it is a tragedy this once beautiful island has been so cruelly ripped apart.

In the evening we had another sixtees night on board but after what we had seen in Phuket no-one really felt much like partying.

DAY SIXTY
Lest We Forget

As a member of Newhaven Royal British Legion I asked Deputy Cruise Director James Gordon if we could arrange a Royal British Legion get-together as I knew there were members of other branches on board.

He arranged it for 11am on day sixty in Andersons bar and there were fifteen members there including myself.

Nine came from Histon in Cambridgeshire and had brought a wreath to lay at Changi Prison and Memorial in Singapore.

There was one from Shipston-on-Stour, one from Whitehaven in Cumbria, I from Wickham in Hampshire and one from Chelmsford.

Ted Hunter belongs to the Chatham-on-Thames branch in Ontario, Canada. He told us there is a population of 50,000 in Chatham and they have two clubs which are soon to amalgamate.

Amanda Wilkins

We had a very interesting meeting exchanging news of all our different branches and a photograph was taken by the Ship's Photographer which I have been asked to send to the Royal British Legion national magazine.

The get-together took over an hour so when I ventured out on to the deck to the barbecue I discovered the temperature was heading for the ninetees. Despite the heat I played cricket in the afternoon and took three wickets. My batting was not so good and I was one of four fielders in our team who dropped catches.

But it was all good fun and we all sweltered together in the heat.

The evening was a mixture of various entertainments, none of which I really wanted to see so I joined one of the opera singers who had just joined the ship to do a series of classical concerts.

Paul Keohone is the baritone with Classical Connections and after we had sailed from Phuket they gave an hour-long performance of operatic arias which received rapturous applause.

We spent a pleasant evening talking opera in the Crows Nest and I went to bed looking forward to their next performance, Golden Greats of the Silver Screen.

DAY SIXTY ONE
There's No Business Like Show Business

Sixty one days out of Southampton produced the best night's entertainment on the cruise.

The daytime was the usual round of shuffleboard and cricket and we had our last tap dancing class for this leg of the cruise.

It was a hilarious session because several of the members had been to the Gold Portunis Club lunch, for which I did not qualify, and had imbibed quite a lot of alcohol so there was a lot of laughter.

I wore my Frank Usher dress for the formal Ladies Night but did not go to the ball. Instead I went to see Classical Connections perform in the Theatre Royal.

Their second programme since they came on board included timeless classics from the movies, and the highlight for me was the duet from The Pearl Fishers sung by tenor Gerraint Dodd and baritone Paul Keohone.

This classical group was a great asset to the cruise and I was delighted they were remaining on board until Southampton.

The timings had been well worked out for the evening so you could see the singers at 10.30pm then go along to the Pacific Lounge at 11.30 to see Denise Nolan give her second and final show.

Sadly she and Tom were getting off the ship the following day to fly home from Colombo.

In this show Denise paid tribute to some of the great ladies of songs, Barbra Streisand, Judy Garland and a great favourite of hers Doris Day.

Because of the early start for several passengers in Sri Lanka the audience was sparse but Denise paid tribute to them saying she had quality not quantity,

This was a first class night of entertainment on board and it is sad we had not had more of them during the nine weeks we had been on board.

Although Denise did not finish until 12.30am as the clocks went back an hour it was not too late when I went to bed. I was not booked on a tour the following morning so I did not have to get up at the crack of dawn.

DAY SIXTY TWO
COLOMBO

The pear-shaped island of Sri Lanka (formerly known as Ceylon) has always been somewhere I would like to visit.

It lies in the Indian Ocean and entirely within the tropics. We berthed early in the Unity Terminal, some thirty five minutes from the town.

I was getting fed up with the ports where you had to travel in by shuttle bus or tender so I decided to walk and experience the real Colombo. I had to get permission from the agent as they are very strict in the port area, no smoking and no photography.

He assured me it would be safe so I set off to walk along the quayside and out of the port gates towards the town.

The first thing that struck me was how dirty and smelly Colombo is and how run down. The town was hit by the tail end of the tsunami and there is evidence of damage along the way. Guards in booths are posted at the worst hit areas and they refused to allow me to take any photographs of either them or the damage.

I left the ship at 8.15am before it got too hot and walked along the perimeter of the port past beautiful gardens.

There was a tiny Buddhist temple which I was allowed to go in to and I remembered to take my shoes off first. It was only big enough to hold two or three people at a time and it was quite delightful.

I had intended to walk right into the town and see the clock tower which was once a lighthouse but I realized I was getting further and further away from the ship.

I was on my own and had not seen a single woman on my travels. The men I passed were all extremely polite and I never felt one ounce of fear. In fact I felt safer in Colombo than I did in England.

Sri Lanka is a similar size to Tasmania and much of the film The Bridge Over the River Quai was filmed there in 1957.

Seventy per cent of the population are Buddhists and in 1960 Mrs Sirima Bandarnaike became the world's first woman prime minister.

When Ceylon became an independent state in 1972 the name was changed to Sri Lanka, Lanka being an old traditional name for the island.

I had originally intended to visit the only elephant orphanage in the world from Colombo but decided against it as it was a nine hour trip. When those on the excursion returned I was very glad I had not gone as they had a two-and-a-half hour coach trip each way with no stops and no toilet on board the coach, some had no air conditioning and the temperature was up in the nineties.

After my two hour walk in the morning I decided to sunbathe on the near deserted ship in the afternoon. I joined entertainment officer Adele who asked me if I could knock down the quayside trader to forty dollars for a leather chair.

After an hour in the sun I went to find the chair and he would not go below sixty dollars and I reported this back to Adele.

My friends back home emailed me to say they had found me a new one bedroom garden flat in Newhaven and I would be moving in the day I got back. I only had a sofa bed and a chest of drawers so Adele and I decided to see if we could get two chairs for one hundred US dollars (£50).

He agreed to this and Adele and I now have a lovely leather chair each for £25. The problem I was faced with when I got home was how to put it all together because the cast iron legs were now separate from the leather seat so that would be my task for the first month after my return.

Those that did venture into the large city were disappointed. I was very glad to have seen the place but I found the squalor similar to the worst parts of Acapulco without the charm of the other half of the seaside resort.

I would have liked to have been there for longer then I could have ventured further afield, to the capital Kandy, 72 miles away, or to Ratnapura, 62 miles, where you pass paddy fields, rubber plantations and tea estates.

That is what Ceylon is famous for and you cannot judge it on one short day in one city the size of Glasgow.

I was exhausted in the evening from my walk and the heat of the day and for the first time on the cruise I went to bed before Janet had even returned to the cabin, which gave her a shock when she walked in

DAY SIXTY THREE
COCHIN

It was my first visit to India and I wasn't disappointed. It was just as I imagined. Beautiful women in colourful saris, hustle and bustle, noise and traffic everywhere.

As we sailed into Cochin in southwest India I marveled at the beautiful scenery.

We passed the long cantilevered fishing nets at the entrance to the harbour which were originally brought to India by Chinese traders from Kublai Khan's court more than a thousand years ago.

We saw the Santa Cruz Roman Catholic basilica in Fort Cochin which is renowned for its beautiful paintings and as we headed for our berth on Willingdon Island we were sandwiched between the neighbouring islands.

Indian crew members excitedly lined the decks looking for their families who had come to meet them and anxiously awaited their landing cards so they could go ashore.

I went ashore with Janet in the morning and bought an Indian rug for my new flat. She was finding the heat a bit overwhelming so we did not venture far. After she decided to return to the ship I experienced the real India as I was now on my own.

I was mobbed by taxi drivers, and drivers of the Auto-rickshaws, the three wheeled vehicles that took passengers into town. These vehicles are not for those of a nervous disposition and I was warned by the Indian ship's agent it was not safe for me to take one on my own.

Indian ladies carrying beads, peacock feather fans and long strings of elephants all came up urging me to buy and beggars carrying young children grabbed me asking for money.

I had planned to walk up the road to the ferry station but I just could not get through the crowds and I returned to the ship for lunch.

After an hour's sunbathing in the afternoon I went ashore with the art teacher Bee Morrison. This was an interesting experience as she would suddenly stop mid-traffic to sketch a palm tree or other interesting site.

On our return to the port we wandered round the stalls

and a young Indian said he wanted my Fossil watch I had bought on board. I handed it over for him to try on and he was thrilled with it.

An ice cream seller in Cochin

Amanda Wilkins

He told me to choose something off his stall and I asked for a large gold wall covering which he refused saying it was worth three hundred American dollars. He went to a pile and got out another one which was like a patchwork quilt.

It had images done in gold thread and mirrors and Bee said it was worth far more than my watch. He asked for one hundred US dollars on top of my watch but I told him I had no more money and asked for it back.

After about five minutes' bartering he held out his hand and said we had a deal so I returned to the ship the proud owner of a lovely Indian wall hanging and he went round his fellow stall holders showing off his new watch.

Before we sailed local entertainers Mohinlyattam came on board to perform Indian dances in the Pacific Lounge. All the girls were beautifully dressed and showed us some lovely dances although I did find the Indian music a bit tedious.

I joined the girls from the Pursers' office to watch us sail out of Cochin which is known as the Venice of the East and you could see why. It is extremely beautiful and a contrast to Mumbai (formerly known as Bombay) which we were due to visit in two days time

DAY SIXTY FOUR
The End of a Leg

As we reached the end of the fourth leg of our World Cruise the temperature was still high and the sun shining down.

At breakfast on deck everyone was intrigued to see a bird hanging on a ledge on the inside of the deck. Cameras, deck cleaners, interested passengers pushing their faces close to it did not disturb it and the bird hung there oblivious to everyone for most of the morning.

The bird hanging on deck.

I went to my usual shuffleboard and on to the musical quiz in the Crow's Nest where I reached a high score for me, thirteen out of twenty. Considering it was a repeat of a quiz we had had on the first leg my marks were pretty abysmal but I just could not remember the previous answers!

I decided to play cricket despite the heat and excelled myself by catching two batsmen out, one of which was from my own bowling!

In the evening Nigel and I were due to have another Night Under the Stars and this time I was determined not to build it up into something it wasn't. We met for a drink before dinner and it was a very relaxed, fun evening. As he had been working all day he had the night off so he was not called away to host some party or other. I had accepted that this was a shipboard romance that just would not happen, he was far too committed to his girlfriend back home and nothing was going to spoil that relationship. I settled for his friendship and we both enjoyed our dinner as much as we had hated the last one.

As he had to be up for Mumbai at 5am the following morning he went to bed quite early and I went to see the Oriana Theatre Company perform the Good Old Bad Old Days for the second time.

This time I took two Union Jacks into the theatre and waved

them high in the air as I sang Land of Hope and Glory with great gusto.

I went to bed far too late for an early morning arrival in Mumbai but I went to bed happy after one of the best evenings I had experienced on the cruise

DAY SIXTY FIVE
MUMBAI
(previously known as Bombay)

I had always wanted to visit India as my father had been stationed there in the army and I was a great fan of the Merchant Ivory films and Jewel in the Crown.

I had enjoyed Cochin but this was the port I was looking forward to. After my late night I did not wake up to see us arrive at 5am. I was woken by Staff Captain Charlie Carr's announcement at 6.15am telling passengers they could proceed ashore.

Mumbai is built on a small island joined to the mainland by an artificial causeway and is a fast-moving international city.

Janet was suffering with a heavy cold but felt well enough to go ashore with me to look round the shops in the terminal building.

We stopped to watch the military band resplendent in their scarlet tunics which reminded me of the days of the Raj before going inside.

I bought a beautiful green and gold sari which fitted me

like a glove and I could not wait to wear it at the next Captain's Welcome Aboard party.

Janet paid for me to have my palm read and I was told I was going to live to a great age, receive a lot of money next year and meet a rich man. When he told me I was going to get married and have four children he lost his credibility as that was an impossibility at my age!

She went back on to the ship and I decided to take a taxi into the town and see the famous Gateway of India. This is Mumbai's main landmark and goes back to the days of sea travel when visiting dignitaries stepped ashore here.

The Gateway of India Mumbai (Bombay)

Amanda Wilkins

Hastily erected in 1911 to mark the visit of King George V and Queen Mary, the arch was properly built in 1927 to commemorate the occasion as it was the first time a reigning monarch had visited India.

My taxi driver spoke very little English and drove a very old Austin Seven. We set off to unknown territory to me and had gone about a mile when he was pulled over by a policeman. The driver offered him money which he refused to take and asked the man to get out of the car and hand over his licence.

Beggars in Mumbai at the Gateway of India

I was getting a bit worried that I would never get back to the ship and had just got out of the cab to find another taxi when he ran back down the road saying "everything was OK." He muttered he had been heavily fined but I never did discover what his offence was.

When we arrived at the Gateway of India I found it a most exciting place. It was full of hustle and bustle and there were snake charmers, peanut sellers, balloon sellers and beggars.

Opposite is the magnificent Taj Mahal hotel with its domes and lovely façade. The beggars did not grab me as they had done in Cochin but some beautiful girls came up and tied jasmine flowers round my wrists and I gave them a dollar each.

Having taken my photographs with my new camera I had a city tour before returning to the ship. Over lunch I was looking at the pictures when I pressed the wrong button and deleted the lot.

I was horrified I had lost all my photographs and after a hasty meal I took another taxi back to the Gateway to take more photographs. This time the snake charmers had disappeared but there was a man who asked if I would like to see his Cobra. He took off the lid of his basket and the snake rose up turning its head to hiss at me.

Amanda Wilkins

The cobra at the Gateway to India

A priest came up and blessed me, patting my head, marking a read dot on my forehead and tying a red and yellow string round my wrist. He pressed some sugar into my hand telling me to eat then asked ten dollars for his temple. Even if he wasn't genuine I found this all part of the excitement of India.

I was sad when we sailed at 5.30pm as I felt this was the best and most exciting port since we had left Australia. It was everything I had hoped for in India and is a place I would love to go back to.

Three hundred passengers got off and new ones on in Mumbai as well as two hundred crew so it was the beginning a the final leg of our mammoth journey.

In the evening the Oriana Theatre Company was performing Follies for the fourth time. I decided I would not see the show again as I had been to it three times and found it very enjoyable. Instead I went to the Casino and lost £20 on blackjack and roulette.

It was whilst I was in the casino I had heard the second show had been cancelled and I later found out that in the first show one of the leading members of the company Chris had been kicked in the head and had fainted.

It was the second incident on board which had been sparked off by the first. A male passenger had a stroke and it was necessary to turn the ship round quickly and get him back to hospital in Mumbai.

Whilst the ship was turning it lurched and in a particularly tricky dance routine in Follies one of the other dancers caught

Amanda Wilkins

Chris on the back of the head.

We lost six hours returning to the Indian port and used a considerable amount of fuel but it was necessary to put the sick passenger ashore as we were facing six days at sea.

DAY SIXTY SIX
Going Home

Following our departure from Mumbai we knew we were really going home. With just over a fortnight to go we would be setting foot on English shores for the first time for three months.

I had mixed feelings as I was looking forward to seeing my friends and my new flat and of course my tiny Yorkshire Terrier but I was not looking forward to returning to temperatures of four degrees.

With three hundred new passengers on board shuffleboard was packed and the games took a long time. I then went and did the individual quiz on alcohol and I was horrified to discover how much I knew, although I didn't win as others knew more!

I played cricket in the afternoon and was thoroughly enjoying being one of the boys and in the evening I attended my fourth Captain's Welcome Aboard party.

This time I went to the First Sitting party as Karl had invited

Janet and I to dine under the stars with him.

Paul from the opera company Classical Connections was joining us and he looked splendid in his kilt whilst I wore my new sari. Sunita, who worked on the reception desk came to my cabin to show me how to put it on correctly and I felt very good wearing it.

We went to the Terrace Bar for a drink before dinner and it was a lovely warm night. This time I had a mixed grill instead of steak and it was delicious. It was sad to think there would not be many more nights when we could dine in the Terrace Grill.

I went to see the new cabaret artist Zoe Tyler after our meal and she was excellent. She had played Fantine in Les Miserables in London and ended her performance with I Dreamed A Dream from the show. Talking to her after the show I discovered she had played Fantine when I first saw the show.

We were now putting the clocks back nearly every night to get us back to Greenwich Mean Time so we were getting an extra hour in bed which was very good news for nightbirds like myself.

DAY SIXTY SEVEN
Round the World in a haze of alcohol

When you want to lose something you win and when you want desperately to win you lose, that's life.

On this particular morning I thought I might just fit in a quick game of shuffleboard before the second Round the World Lunch. As it started at 10 am given my current record I thought I would be out by 11.15am.

But as luck would have it my partner John and I kept winning, even when we were 33-18 down in the third of four ends.

We eventually got beaten in the semi final at 11.40am and I had twenty minutes to get showered and changed for the cocktail party and lunch.

I just made it and after another sumptuous meal, four glasses of wine and a glass of port I decided to play cricket. I play better after alcohol as I was hitting out with the bat at random with no inhibitions and my bowling was spot on.

I then went to tap dancing and as three of us had attended the lunch it was the most light-hearted session we had been to and I felt sorry for the newcomers who had just joined the class.

Despite a large lunch I still felt hungry at dinner time and managed a three course meal before reviewing the evening's entertainment.

I really wanted to see the comedian Allan Stewart as he had been on Arcadia when I cruised before and he is very funny. But Elizabeth and Les Leggett, who I had teamed up with for the two previous editions of Call My Bluff wanted me to join them.

They were a sweet couple and I felt it was my duty to do so. The team had changed from the previous sessions and there were very few people watching as they were all in the theatre. But I was glad I went. One thing I had learnt on my travels was you had to give and take on a World Cruise and the "all-rounders" had to look out for each other.

If you didn't do that you would have a miserable time like the Dutch lady who spent the first ten days shut in her cabin and eventually gave up and flew home from Hong Kong. Going round the world in one ship with eight hundred other passengers for three months is not easy. You cannot get away until you reach port but if you make allowances and don't let the stress overtake you then for ninety-nine per cent of the time the cruise is a wonderful experience.

I had bad days but those were of my own making. I allowed homesickness, depression and loneliness to sit on my shoulder for a couple of days but it soon passed and there are plenty of people on the ship to help you through the bad times.

DAY SIXTY EIGHT
Dinner in Focus

By this stage of the cruise I had become bored with my routine of playing shuffleboard in the morning and cricket in the afternoon.

A number of passengers had recently started dislocating fingers and getting bruised shins from the hard rubber ball used in the deck cricket and I was beginning to wonder if it was such a good idea.

Oriana Theatre Company staged a special matinee of Follies to replace the cancelled performance and I decided to see it for the fourth time. It was one of their best shows and included a charming scene of Irish dancing and singing.

It was nice to see Chris Southgate dancing and singing as well as ever following his accident and I sent him a small teddy bear from the shop to welcome him back.

In the evening I joined the three photographers who had been on the ship since January 7 for dinner under the stars.

We were a mixed bunch with myself from England, Christiana from Italy and Ashley and his fiancé Julie from Australia.

It was a very nice relaxed evening and none of us talked photography all evening. I learnt that Julie and Ashley had met working for the Australian end of BTCV the conservation group which has a branch in England. I had been on four conservation holidays with them and I knew they had branches all over the world.

Julie and Ashley are planning to get married on a houseboat in Australia in April 2006 and work together on the ship because they love to travel.

We stayed on deck till late on a lovely balmy evening with just the lights from the candles on the tables and the lapping of the sea against the side of the ship. It was hard to believe that in just two weeks' time we would be back in the cold English climate.

DAY SIXTY NINE
St Patrick's Day

Oriana went green on the sixty ninth day of the cruise in honour of the Irish passengers. Mavis Bee, the handicraft lecturer made a point of teaching people to make shamrocks and several people walked round in green rugby shirts.

Angie Carr, the Captain's wife wore a sweatshirt with Guinness across the front and that drink was the order of the day.

Passengers get tetchy when they near home but some incidents are more funny than serious. I was scoring for a game of shuffleboard on deck thirteen when the Chief Petty Officer came along with two seamen and told me the court had to be painted. I asked him to wait until the end of the game and I advised him when we had finished.

I told the entertainment officer Carole that they had said it was allocated for painting and she said she had told them not to start. I had just begun my own game when an irate passenger came storming round the corner.

"Amanda, did you tell them to start painting?" she said. I assured her I hadn't but when I finished my game I went round the corner to be faced by other angry passengers who blamed me for the chaos caused by sixty passengers having to play a competition on three courts instead of four.

I was glad to have a nice relaxed lunch with my purser friends and forget the fiasco of the shuffleboard courts.

I had been extremely lucky with my third table on this cruise as all my companions were very nice and amusing. Dinner was now a pleasure instead of a chore and the menu was predominantly Irish on March 17.

Oriana Theatre Company were presenting Fosse which I had seen three times before so I opted for the Irish night in Lords Tavern listening to all the old favourites including Danny Boy.

We had celebrated Burns Night, St David's Day and St Patrick's Day on board and I felt it was a shame we would not be on board for St George's Day in April.

DAY SEVENTY
Ten Days to Go

Despite the fact we were now nearing home we woke up to one of the hottest days we had had.

We were now in the Red Sea heading for Egypt and there was a warm breeze that stopped the temperatures soaring even higher.

I played my usual game of shuffleboard and in the afternoon I decided to enter the Celebrity Blackjack Tournament in the Casino.

The entry fee was £5 and you received £1000 worth of chips to gamble on seven deals. Eight people who won the most money in the qualifying rounds went through to the final to win £100.

I was surprised to find my dealer was none other than the Captain Mike Carr and he took great pleasure in taking all my chips I had gambled on my final deal. It was all good fun and like the loser in the Weakest Link final I went home with nothing.

The opera singers, Classical Connections presented Top Hats and Tiaras before dinner which included Un Bel Di from Madame Butterfly and the Flower Duet from Lakme which is now the theme for the British Airways advertisement.

I decided to watch Zoe Tyler's show in the Theatre Royal after dinner and was very glad I did. She began work in the West End at the age of eighteen when she played the role of Fantine in Les Miserables.

Other hit musicals followed including Jesus Christ Superstar, Fame and her favourite role of the Gospel Singer in Smokey Joe's Café.

She gave a great performance which included the Eva Cassidy hit Fields of Gold and songs from Sunset Boulevard. I bought her CD after the show which she signed for me but several of us realized afterwards that we had all bought them and none of us had asked the price. We just signed the order placed via our cruise card but that is why shipboard life is so unreal.

My musical evening ended with the Jeff Wraight Trio giving us some superb jazz in the Crow's Nest. They are the resident musicians on Aurora but as she was still undergoing repairs following her breakdown they had been flown out to join Oriana which was a bonus for us.

DAY SEVENTY ONE
SHARM EL-SHEIKH

After this port I changed my opinion of Egypt. I had only visited the country once before when I cruised to Alexandria and I found it dirty and depressing.

The small town of Sharm el-Sheikh, and its near neighbour Naama Bay, was hit by terrorist attacks four months after I visited the place.

We docked a short distance from Sharm el-Sheikh and Janet and I took the ship's bus into Naama Bay.

This is a very recent creation and we could see as we drove there the extensive building work that is still going on. It was 7km (4.5 miles) from Sharm el-Sheikh and it is essentially a one-street resort of hotels, restaurants and shops.

It has grown from virtually nothing in the early 1980s to become the leading resort in the southern Sinai Peninsula.

I had never seen so many hubble bubble pipes in my life and I bought one for my new flat.

We went to a restaurant where I had an Irish coffee and Janet had a Nescafe before looking round the town again.

Our coach was not due to return to the ship until 2.30pm so we went to a beach restaurant where we hired two sunbeds under an umbrella with new towels for seven US dollars for the two.

Janet on the beach in Naama Bay

I found the Red Sea too cold to swim in so I just paddled then we were served lunch at our beds

Entering into the holiday spirit I decided to let a young Egyptian give me a henna tattoo for eight dollars. I chose a small picture of Cleopatra but I was horrified to find when he had finished it was two inches long.

80 Days at Sea

The Author getting her tattoo on the beach

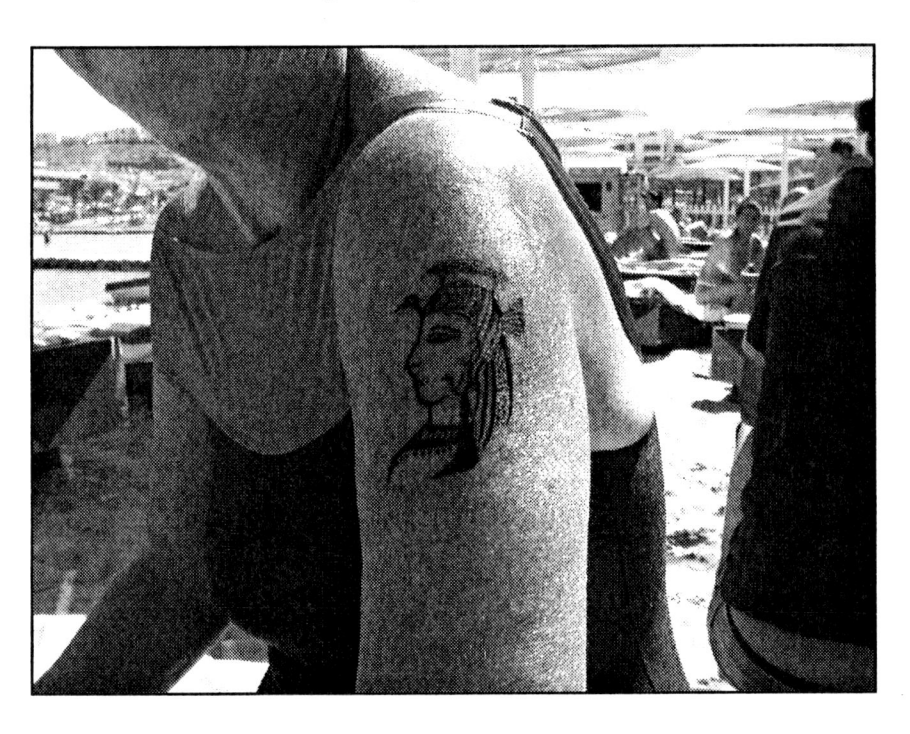

It was not permanent but I was told it would last ten days to a fortnight – long enough to shock my friends back home.

I found Naama Bay to be a lovely place and I certainly wouldn't mind returning there on holiday.

The coach, run by the Egyptians, was very comfortable and efficient and picked us up on time. The drive to and from the ship was very pretty and it was certainly a port I thoroughly enjoyed.

To round off a very pleasant day I went to the special Asian Buffet Dinner in the Conservatory. The starters were plentiful and I felt extremely full as I waddled down to bed in preparation for our transit through the Suez Canal the following day.

DAY SEVENTY TWO
Suez Canal Transit

I decided not to get off the ship at 4am to go to Cairo to see the Pyramids as I had already done that from Alexandria several years ago.

Instead I remained on board and got up at 5.50am to see us go through the Suez Canal. It was very interesting to note the contrast between the Panama Canal and the Suez Canal and I was very lucky to have experienced them both in one trip.

The canal runs from Egypt to the Mediterranean through the Bitter Lakes and the two banks are completely different.

On the starboard side was the Sinai Desert whilst on the port side there were expensive houses, fields and plantations.

Suez is at the Red Sea end and Port Said is at the Mediterranean end of the Suez Canal and it is guarded at various check points on both sides by the military who are terrified of a terrorist invasion via the canal.

Transitting the Suex Canal

I stood on deck with Paula who was travelling with the art lecturer Bee Morrison and we had great fun watching the soldiers through our binoculars, waving to them and getting them to wave back.

Once during the morning I was on deck on my own in a bikini top and brief shorts. I waved to a soldier standing in the doorway of his post and I heard a lot of whistling. I saw him running up the sandy hill till he reached a jeep where he was handed a pair of binoculars which were immediately trained on me.

I realized afterwards they would not have seen many

women with their knees and top of their shoulders exposed and I thought I had never had so much fun in my life.

Suez Canal

It took all of a day to transit the canal and it was so much more interesting than Panama. That was beautiful but there was so much to see in this second canal.

We saw a camel train, nomads, two men riding donkeys, lots of workers and soldiers and some lovely houses, including the two homes owned by the President.

We docked at Port Said at 5.40pm to pick up the passengers who had made the thirteen-and-a-half hour trip to Cairo and back.

The Egyptian Immigration officials allowed passengers to go ashore on to the quay to visit the various stalls that had been set up and I bought a few presents to take home.

It was a shame we were not allowed outside the port gates as the town looked very interesting. Founded in 1869 it currently has a population of one million people, many of whom are concerned with the Suez Canal.

It is built on a sandy peninsula extending between Menzalah Lake and the African Western Bank of the Suez Canal.

The journey from Cairo takes three-and-a-half hours and we were supposed to be in port for just an hour, between 6pm and 7pm. But two of the coaches were an hour late getting back to the ship and the refuelling of oil took longer than expected so we did not leave Port Said until 9.20pm.

By then it had turned very cold so we watched our departure from the picture window in the restaurant as we ate our dinner.

For me this was really the end of my world trip as the next two ports of call, Athens and Barcelona, were very familiar to me. I was sad that my trip of a lifetime was coming to an end but had no regrets about having undertaken such a mammoth journey.

DAY SEVENTY THREE
You Are The Weakest Link.

This was the day I was to be a member of the passenger team in Don't Break the Chain – Oriana's version of The Weakest Link.

Apprehension about the forthcoming show affected my shuffleboard and I crashed out in the first round on a very windy day.

I was unable to concentrate on anything in the afternoon and wondered why I had volunteered to be one of the seven man team.

I chose to wear black velvet trousers and a black velvet top under one of my Chinese silk jackets I had purchased at Port Klang. Nigel came to the Crow's Nest bar to give me moral support before dinner and at 10pm I reported to the Cruise Director's office for my briefing.

As my name began with A I had to walk on first and when the lights dimmed and I faced the spotlights it was quite frightening.

I was handed the microphone and answered the first question correctly and at the end of the four minute round I couldn't believe I had only got one question wrong.

Confident that I would last at least one round I was amazed when four of my fellow contestants voted me off first. It was obviously a conspiracy cooked up by the eventual finalists, the husband and wife team, and their best friend.

The one thing I had dreaded was to have to do the first walk of shame and there I was doing it.

I had to be interviewed on the video camera and I was quite honest and said I didn't believe I should have been voted off first.

It was surprising how many passengers I had never spoken to before came up to me and said they felt I shouldn't have been voted off first.

That was encouraging for me and I was very glad I had agreed to do it. The contest finished in time for me to see the end of the very funny comedian Allan Stewart and I was sorry it was his last show.

After the theatre I joined the contest winner and runners up for a drink to show there were no hard feelings but I felt it was not something I would volunteer for again – like the Fun in the Sun on the greasy pole. I just put it down to experience.

DAY SEVENTY FOUR
Piraeus for Athens

As I had been to Athens numerous times before I decided not to travel the five miles into the city from the port of Piraeus.

Instead, I remained in the port and explored the town. Piraeus is now the communication centre for the whole of Greece and its extensive docks control trade in and out of the country.

It has shipyards, factories and a refinery and is the main focus for all the ferries to and from the Greek Islands.

The temperature had dropped considerably and I went ashore in cords, a sweatshirt and a fleece.

My first stop was at the Church of St Nicholas, a short walk from the ship. It has impressive blue domes and marble steps up to the entrance.

When I went inside I was confronted by the beauty of it all. Large gold chandeliers, painted icons and candles burning brightly. I lit a candle for my late mother and I spent some time in the church as it was a very peaceful place.

The Church of St Nicholas Pireaus

Piraeus is an interesting place to walk round with the contrast of the modern marina and the busy streets where an old Greek woman was begging.

The sun came out at one point but after lunch it turned cold again and I stayed on the ship to go to the cinema to see a strange film called Phone Booth.

Starring Colin Farrell and Kiefer Sutherland it told the story of a man trapped in a public phone booth by a sniper who said he would be killed if he hung up the receiver and left the box.

I had decided to give a party in the evening to thank everyone who had supported me throughout the three month trip. Nigel organized it for me and I held it in the Medina Room.

Oriana in Piraeus

I invited some of the officers, passengers from my three tables, the opera singers and other friends I had made.

It is unusual to enjoy your own party but I found it a lovely evening and was very pleased my guests felt the same. A hurried dinner followed as I was to make my second appearance as a model.

This time I had four changes of clothes from the Knightsbridge Shop, a casual top and shorts, a reversible dress, a £400 silk trouser suit and a beautiful black and white velvet evening dress.

It was lovely to be able to wear beautiful clothes I could not afford and we had fun doing the show which was held this time in the Pacific Lounge.

Comedian Tom O'Connor had come on board in Athens and was scheduled to do a show the next day. But one of the theatre company was taken ill which meant their show had to be cancelled so Tom did his show at the same time as the fashion show.

Not only did it deplete our audience, it meant I was only able to catch the end of it which was a shame as he is very funny.

DAY SEVENTY FIVE
The cold cold wind of home

On this morning just five days from English waters we noticed a real change in the weather.

The sea was grey, the skies cloudy and the wind was cold. People valiantly tried to play shuffleboard wrapped up in fleeces with hoods and thick trousers as none of us wanted to admit the hot weather was a thing of the past.

The individual quiz had been moved inside to the Lords Tavern instead of being held by the swimming pool and few people attended.

After lunch I ventured inside to play table tennis but lack of practice meant I came out in the first round.

A group of passengers had been working very hard on songs from Gilbert and Sullivan and some of my table were involved. With a heavy heart I went to the Pacific Lounge to watch as I am not a great fan of Gilbert and Sullivan and I was agreeably surprised at their performance.

I had to change quickly for dinner as Ton O'Connor had invited me for a drink in the Crows Nest at 7pm. We had met on the Arcadia and again in Eastbourne when he compered the RAF Band Christmas Concert.

We spent an hour together before he had to go to the Captain's Cocktail Party and I have never met a more charming man. He was amusing and entertaining company and I was sorry when the Captain's deck called.

Because of the re-scheduling of the entertainment the previous night the only thing to see that night was There's No Business Like Show Business.

The Oriana Theatre Company were very good but the consistent repeats of the shows since Sydney were irritating several Round the World passengers. I love theatre but even I was getting tired of seeing the same show four times.

They performed it very well but somehow it had lost the zest of the first showing and it was unfair on the company who are as good as ever. I had thought the entertainment on a World Cruise would be very special. Perhaps it was in the heyday of cruising but now the World Cruise is treated as five separate legs and repeats are the norm.

P & O do take passengers' comments very seriously and I hope they will listen to the observations from a number of

Round the World passengers about the entertainment and it will be rectified before next year's World Cruise.

DAY SEVENTY SIX
Tom O'Connor holds court

Just before 11am on day seventy six I was invited by Tom O'Connor to have my photograph taken with him for my book.

He told be to go backstage at the Theatre Royal in my best frock so I put on my prettiest lace blouse and a summer skirt.

What I had not been told was the stage door was on the open deck at the back of the theatre and I had to battle through a biting wind in a sleeveless top to get there.

For more than an hour Tom kept the audience enthralled with tales of his early life. He was the first comedian on Oriana's maiden voyage ten years ago and he has been in show business for thirty years.

"I always wanted to be a docker as my dad was a docker," he said, "But my dad wanted me to be a priest and my mother wanted me to be a doctor."

They lived in a two up, two down house in Bootle with a parlour and a back kitchen. Tom's father weighed twenty two stone and his mother was very religious and played the piano.

The author with Tom O'Connor

"She thought she was very good but actually she played the piano like Les Dawson," he said.

His first job was working as a docker unloading coffee beans and it was whilst working in the docks he first realized you don't have to tell jokes to be funny.

"My boss was called Harry the Horse, I don't know why," he said. "One day he disappeared and someone came looking for him. One of the dockers said they hadn't seen head nor tail of him for days."

Tom trained as a teacher and met his wife Pat at training college in Twickenham. She had three babies in quick succession and couldn't work so Tom started singing and playing guitar in the pubs with Brendon McCormack who is now a well known guitarist.

"We were called Tom and Brennie and our local butcher was our manager and drove us round in his van," he said. "We sat in the back where all the meat hung up."

Tom picked up his stories as he went along and said he got one from a lady in the audience.

"She told me about a funeral where people were gathered round the grave throwing earth on to the coffin. Then the widow came up with a large china horse which she threw into the grave smashing it into pieces. "Try and back that each way if you can," she said."

He says you don't have to be rude to be funny and has always given a clean family act. It was because of that Hughie Green invited him on to Opportunity Knocks and he won it three weeks running.

On his last appearance Bernard Delfont was in the audience and chose Tom to appear as a regular in the TV show Name That Tune which gave him his big break.

He said it gave him instant stardom and it was quite scary to get taxi drivers calling out Hello Tom to him whenever they saw him.

He has always been popular with all age groups and has only once had a complaint about a joke he told.

"The one subject you cannot joke about is the Titanic," he said. "I was doing my show on television and had Roger de Courcey and Nookie Bear as my guest. I was desperate for a bear joke and I asked Bill Oddie if he had any.

"He gave me one which I liked and I said there were a group of people outside the White Star building the day after the Titanic went down.

"A man was reading the list of survivors and watching at the back was a polar bear. He shouted out "any news of the iceburg?"

Tom said the television company killed the joke immediately and he has never told any Titanic jokes since.

He received a standing ovation after the interviews then happily stood around talking to passengers afterwards.

It was sad he was on the ship for such a short time as he was due to fly home the next day from Barcelona.

DAY SEVENTY SEVEN
Good Friday in Barcelona.

Our last port of call was Barcelona, the progressive capital of Catalunya. It is a thriving port and the most prosperous commercial centre in Spain.

We were berthed very near the town and P & O laid on a shuttle bus which took less than ten minutes to drop as at the bottom of the Ramblas.

It is a very beautiful city and as it was Good Friday there was plenty of activity. An antique fair was spread along the sea front and amazing living statues were spaced along the Ramblas dressed in weird and wonderful costumes.

A number of street artists were doing portraits and caricatures of people and I had mine done by a young Chinese man. It was not very flattering ss he gave me ears like Prince Charles, but I could see the.likeness as caricatures are meant to be cruel.

Living Statues in The Ramblas, Barcelona

I spent a long time walking round the town which I had visited before and I would certainly like to visit again.

I returned to the ship for lunch and then returned to the town in the afternoon. I visited the impressive cathedral situated in the heart of the Barri Goric and surrounded by many beautiful squares and buildings.

The cathedral was begun in 1298 by Jaume II but the western façade was only completed in 1892.

As the shuttle bus brought me back to the ship for the last time I felt very sad that this was to be my home for only another three days. Although I had suffered pangs of homesickness now I realized how much I was going to miss it and all my friends on board.

Living Statues in The Ramblas, Barcelona

As we sailed out of our last port before Southampton addresses were beginning to be exchanged and there was a sadness around the deck as the lights of Barcelona faded into the distance.

I had hoped the last few days and nights would be really fun so that I would get off the ship with great sadness. But they weren't. People were getting stressed and my real friends, apart from Janet, had got off the ship weeks ago.

People asked my if I would be sad to leave "my officer" as Nigel and I had been seen around together so much. But I knew he never had been "my officer" and had no more interest in me than any other passengers he had sailed with on previous cruises.

I wanted to dance but there was no-one to dance with and the the disco was empty. Rounding off a frustrating day and night I turned on an innocent young entertainment officer and told her "I can't wait to get off this bloody ship!"

DAY SEVENTY EIGHT
The end is nigh

The weather deteriorated and we had to don warm clothes. I knew we were almost home when I put the television on in the cabin and I got an episode of the daily soap Doctors on the BBC.

I spent the morning packing and wondered how I was going to get everything in. The Staff Captain had sent me down some rope and I wrapped my Tongan carving in a towel and bound it up to send off with my luggage.

Janet and I had our first clash in three months when we both tried to pack together and we realized we were going to have to work out a rota.

I pulled down the upper bunk above my bed to store my packed suitcase so I could get the other one out of the hold and put it under my bed.

At 4pm we had our tap class and worked hard on our routine we had to perform on the last night. We had all come on leaps and bounds since we started and were now doing a much longer and more complicated dance.

We passed the Rock of Gibraltar at 6.45pm and were within three miles so we had a clear view of Europa Point. I remembered when my mother and I had spent a fortnight there after my father died and how much I had enjoyed the place.

The Captain warned us we would hit a heavy swell once we had passed through the Straits of Gibraltar into the Atlantic and we certainly moved around as I sat in the Oriental Restaurant trying to eat dinner.

I did not feel seasick but my head felt very heavy and and I wanted to go to sleep. As soon as I left the restaurant I felt better and I spent a very happy hour having a farewell drink with Nigel in the Crows Nest bar. I knew I was going to miss his company and hoped he would keep in touch, but I knew I would not hear from him again.

At 11.30pm we went down to the Pacific Lounge to watch Oriana Theatre Company perform Pop Parade. It was the one production they had not performed much and it was a very good fast-moving show.

It was with a heavy heart I went to bed knowing I had only a few more nights in the cabin which had become my home. It was going to be strange adapting to normal life again and

Amanda Wilkins

although I was looking forward to seeing my friends I had got over my previous night's frustration and I knew I would miss the ship.

DAY SEVENTY NINE
EASTER SUNDAY

The sea was very rough and we had to hold on to anyone and anything to walk along the deck.

Indoor activities were the order of the day and I went to the Easter Service in the Theatre Royal taken by Captain Mike Carr.

I was just packing one of my cases when there was a knock at the cabin door and I opened it to receive a silver tray bearing a chocolate Easter Egg filled with Belgian chocolates.

It was from Nigel and the food and beverage department and was a complete surprise. It was the first present of the day as later the girls on the reception desk gave me a World Cruise teddy bear and a notebook and pen inscribed with messages from all of them.

I had made some very good friends on the ship and I was going to miss them. I bought a teddy bear bearing a rose from the shop and enlisted the help of one of the purser's department

The surprise delivered to the author's cabin on Easter Sunday

Mario who promised to give it to Nigel when the ship sailed out of Southampton on the night we disembarked. I knew he would probably be embarrassed by my present but by the time he received it I would be miles away from Oriana. A few days after I arrived home I regretted this gesture but I have always been an impulsive person.

The Captain gave farewell cocktail parties on the last formal night of the cruise and I went round saying goodbye to people I might not see on the final day.

After dinner the farewell ball was one of the best dances

they had on the ship. Packed with passengers all out to enjoy themselves we did several novelty dances where there were enough partners for everyone.

I went to the midnight cabaret by vocalist Chris Ritchie and I was very sorry for him as he had a very small audience but as he said he had quality not quantity.

He was very good and was my type of singer as his programme included Love Changes Everything from Aspects of Love and the Nat King Cole hit Unforgettable.

I had to bite back the tears as I walked down the corridor because I realized the next day we would be in English waters and back home to reality.

DAY EIGHTY
The Final Chapter

The last day was a nightmare. I had to buy two extra bags to get the stuff in I had bought and Janet and I had to organize a rota as we couldn't both pack at the same time.

The weather was wet and windy and every time someone came up to say goodbye the floodgates opened.

We had become a family in the three months we had been together and it was sad to bid farewell to new-found friends knowing we were unlikely to see them again.

Nigel and I had a last drink together in the Crow's Nest bar with me sitting on the stool that had become mine for the voyage. He was late due to pressure of work so by the time he arrived I was in a strop and it was not the farewell I had hoped for.

After dinner the Oriana Tappers gave a display of the latest dance routine we had worked so hard at with Elaine.

I knew I was going to miss Nigel and Janet the most and although we all said we would keep in touch I knew that I would probably not see either of them again.

We arrived back at Southampton in the rain and were greeted with the news that the conveyor belt carrying the luggage had broken down and disembarkation was delayed by over an hour.

People sat around with their luggage on any seat they could find as we all had to be out of our cabins so they could prepare for the new passengers coming on board.

Eventually I got off to be met by my good friends Geoff and Pam Nichols who had driven me down and I felt very strange being back in England.

I had traveled the world in eighty days visiting countries I had only ever dreamed off. For three months I had lived in fantasy land and now I had arrived back to face reality.

I knew it would take a few days to adjust and be able to cope but I was determined to retain the confidence Nigel had given me and live up to his final words – "keep smiling, be positive.

EPILOGUE

Almost six months to the day I first saw him singing Don Jose in Sydney Opera House I met Julian Gavin.

Tenor Julian Gavin

He was singing the part of Jenik in The Bartered Bride at Glyndebourne Opera House, half an hour from where I live and I asked if we could meet up.

He invited me along on the last night of the production and I was lucky enough to get myself a return ticket for the performance.

Born in Melbourne Julian trained as a conductor and clarinetist and he taught clarinet at Melbourne University.

In his mid-20s he decided he wanted to become an opera singer and he moved his family to England so he could study at the National Opera Studio.

I asked him why he would want to leave the sunny climes of Australia for a home in Coulsdon, near Purley.

"When I finished my training there were far more opportunities at different levels," he said. "There are more touring companies and I do get to go back to Australia fairly regularly to sing."

So what is the difference between Glyndebourne and Sydney Opera Houses?

"It is hard to compare the two," he said. "Glyndebourne is very special, there is nothing like it in the world.

"Once you are working inside Sydney Opera House it is not unlike any other building. The first sight of it is breathtaking and the dressing rooms must have the best views anywhere as they all look out over the harbour."

Julian said it is wonderful when you are singing there to

walk across to the botanical gardens but most of the rehearsals are up in Surrey Hills in Elizabeth Street and they only move into the opera house at the last minute.

"At Glyndebourne we have long rehearsal periods in a rural environment with the sheep bleating outside. We just love England and we have gone for British as well as Australian citizenship."

Julian's five children have made their lives over here and the eldest is about to go to university.

"The thing about Sydney is there is so much variety with the audiences," he said. "One week you get the cruise ships in bringing a party, the next it is something different.

"We have a marvellous theatre in Melbourne as well and the joke over there is Australia now has its opera house – the exterior is in Sydney and the interior is in Melbourne!"

Julian's interview and his contrasting performance in an opera set in post-war Czechoslovakia was the icing on the cake as far as my story is concerned.

A story which began with the helpful staff at Personal Service Travel in Eastbourne and ended with the look of horror on the faces of my friends Pam and Geoff Nichols when they saw the amount of luggage I brought back.

Would I do the trip again? I would go back to all the places tomorrow if I had the money but I would do it in stages so I could spend more time in each of them. But if this book has proved anything – it is never too late to follow your dream.

For Roy —
with every good
wish always
Colin Dexter